MW01671504

# EVERYDAY VOCABULARY

# EveryDay Vocabulary

*Laurie Rozakis, Ph.D.*

MADISON PARK PRESS™
NEW YORK

Copyright © 1998 by Byron Preiss Visual Publications, Inc.

All rights reserved. No part of this publication may be reproduced, stored in a retrieval system, or transmitted, in any form or by any means, electronic, mechanical, photocopying, recording, or otherwise, without the prior permission of the publishers.

Published by Madison Park Press, 15 East 26th Street, New York, NY 10010. Madison Park Press is a trademark of Bookspan.

Book design by Pearl Lau

ISBN: 978-1-58288-282-6

Printed in the United States of America

# TABLE OF CONTENTS

# INTRODUCTION

*President Calvin Coolidge once invited friends from his hometown to dine at the White House. Worried about their table manners, the guests decided to do everything that Coolidge did. This strategy succeeded—until coffee was served. The president poured his coffee into the saucer. The guests did the same. Coolidge added sugar and cream. His guests did, too. Then Coolidge bent over and put his saucer on the floor for the cat.*

Ever feel like those poor guests? Does it seem like you don't know how to act because your vocabulary doesn't quite measure up? Have you decided that it's time to improve your vocabulary? Put a check next to each statement that applies to your feelings about vocabulary.

______ 1. I feel frustrated because I don't always understand some of the words that people use in daily conversation.

______ 2. My career has suffered because of my weak vocabulary.

______ 3. I know I need to improve my vocabulary, but I just don't have the time for formal study.

______ 4. I could do better on standardized tests if I had a stronger vocabulary.

______ 5. English isn't my first language, so I don't know as much English as I would like.

______ 6. I sometimes have trouble understanding what I read because I don't know what all the words mean.

______ 7. I know that I have to learn more English to be competitive, especially in the twenty-first century.

______ 8. I would feel better about myself if I had a stronger vocabulary.

Many people just like you want to learn how to communicate more effectively in English. That's because they know that better language skills will help them succeed in school, at work, and in their personal lives. Help is on the way.

So what if you never read the letters in your alphabet soup? So what if attention to detail isn't your strong suit? You can still master an impressive number of useful vocabulary words. Hey, I did, and I still can't program a VCR, complete a withdrawal from an ATM, or make my kids understand the meaning of the word, "no." But I improved my vocabulary—and so can you.

Work your way through the lessons in this book and you'll feel a great deal more confident when it comes to expressing yourself in speech and writing.

## TEST YOUR VOCABULARY

To see how your vocabulary measures up to that of other people, take the following vocabulary test. As you work, put a check next to any word you don't know. After you complete the test, see which of your choices were correct. Then take a few minutes to study the words you missed.

The test contains twenty-five phrases, each containing an underlined word. Write the letter of the correct response in the space indicated. Take as much time as you need.

_______ 1. a <u>gaudy</u> piece of jewelry

a. flashy c. colorless
b. plain d. expensive

_______ 2. a <u>prevalent</u> condition

a. rare c. childhood
b. contagious d. common

_______ 3. a <u>somber</u> event

a. joyous c. exhilarated
b. unexpected d. gloomy

_______ 4. a <u>loquacious</u> person

a. nasty c. talkative
b. violent d. quiet

_______ 5. a <u>lenient</u> teacher

a. not strict c. demanding
b. austere d. attractive

_______ 6. a <u>vicarious</u> thrill

a. painful c. empathetic
b. unexpected d. innocent

_______ 7. an <u>ominous</u> event

a. portentous c. facetious
b. impulsive d. incomparable

_______ 8. an <u>audacious</u> undertaking

a. tricky c. bold
b. sly d. cowardly

_______ 9. a prosaic book

a. mundane
b. extraordinary
c. bizarre
d. tattered

_______ 10. a latent aptitude

a. conspicuous
b. pliable
c. dangerous
d. potential

_______ 11. a vernacular language

a. elevated
b. native
c. hard to understand
d. hard to spell

_______ 12. an imminent warning

a. late
b. impending
c. incomplete
d. protracted

_______ 13. a disheveled home

a. untidy
b. neat
c. protected
d. well-tended

_______ 14. a religious icon

a. belief
b. value
c. statement
d. symbol or image

_______ 15. a vivacious performer

a. aged
b. off-color
c. lively
d. overrated

_______ 16. inclement weather

a. harsh
b. rare
c. pleasant
d. balmy

ENGLISH HAS MORE THAN ONE MILLION WORDS.

_______ 17. a baffling situation

a. enjoyable
b. dismal
c. clear
d. confusing

_______ 18. a lackluster report

a. verbose
b. long
c. dull, colorless
d. thrilling

_______ 19. a caustic comment

a. surprising c. biting
b. complimentary d. witty

_______ 20. to feign illness

a. suffer c. die from
b. pretend d. enjoy

_______ 21. to cajole someone

a. insult c. wheedle
b. scorn d. ignore

_______ 22. a timely caveat

a. article of clothing c. pet
b. bargain d. warning

_______ 23. a hiatus in programming

a. extension c. continuation
b. sequel d. gap

_______ 24. a cavalier attitude

a. polite c. serious
b. disdainful d. humorous

_______ 25. an agile gymnast

a. clumsy c. ungainly
b. limber d. injured

### Answers

| | |
|---|---|
| 1. a | 14. d |
| 2. d | 15. c |
| 3. d | 16. a |
| 4. c | 17. d |
| 5. a | 18. c |
| 6. c | 19. c |
| 7. a | 20. b |
| 8. c | 21. c |
| 9. a | 22. d |
| 10. d | 23. d |
| 11. b | 24. b |
| 12. b | 25. b |
| 13. a | |

## ✔ Score Yourself

16–20 correct: Superior (Go to the head of the class).
11–15 correct: Above average (This should be a piece of cake).
6–10 correct: Average (We should talk).
0–5 correct: Below average (You need me, you really need me).

## Note to Reader

In nearly all cases, the most common definitions are used for the vocabulary words in this book. Some of the words, however, have more than one meaning. When in doubt, always consult your dictionary.

# PART I:

# VOCABULARY TIPS

**• • • •**

***A person went to a restaurant and ordered a sandwich. She asked the server behind the counter for minimal lettuce. He said he was sorry, but they only had iceberg lettuce.***

Words are the building blocks of thought. They are the way we understand the ideas of others and express our own opinions. It's only logical then that people who know how to use words accurately find it easier to achieve their aims—in this case, to get a sandwich without too much lettuce.

In the first section of this book, you'll learn some effective and fun ways to pump up your everyday vocabulary. You'll learn how to expand your vocabulary in just a few minutes a day, often in less time than it takes to get a sandwich the way you want it.

# CHAPTER 1

# IN THE KNOW:

# TRICKS OF THE TRADE

YOU MUST REMEMBER THIS

Want to pump up your vocabulary? Don't despair! Instead, try some easy tricks of the vocabulary trade. This chapter covers ten proven methods. Here they are:

Pronounce words correctly.
Use word cards.
Learn synonyms and antonyms.
Understand a word's unstated meanings.
Break a word into smaller parts that you can decode easily.
Use a print dictionary and an on-line thesaurus.
Create mnemonics (memory tricks) to help you differentiate between confusing words.
Use context clues.
Learn word histories.
Use newly learned words in your conversation and writing.

ALL THE RIGHT MOVES

There are so many tried-and-true ways to improve your vocabulary that you're sure to find several that work for you. Reading a lot will always help.

Want a more effective and powerful vocabulary? Well, you can memorize lists of words, and there's nothing wrong with that—except it's so *boring*. As a result, even people with the best intentions soon decide that they have better things to do than stare at word lists. (And they usually do!)

To unlock the secret to a wide and useful vocabulary, you need to do more than memorize lists of words. Rather, your goal should be to

• develop a system that will help you remember the vocabulary words you'll learn; and

• increase your chances of correctly defining and using many other words that you've yet to encounter.

The following guidelines can help you develop just such a strategy to reach these goals. Whatever your level of skill, you can benefit from the following time-tested vocabulary techniques. They're easy—and they work.

To get the greatest benefit from this section, read the guidelines through several times. Practice them with the vocabulary words given in this chapter. Then use the guidelines as you work your way through this book.

THE OXFORD ENGLISH DICTIONARY LISTS MORE THAN 500,000 WORDS; GERMAN HAS FEWER THAN ONE-THIRD THAT NUMBER, FRENCH FEWER THAN ONE-SIXTH.

## YOU SAY PO-TAY-TOE AND I SAY PO-TAT-TOE: PRONOUNCE WORDS CORRECTLY

Knowing the meaning of a word is only half the battle; you also have to know how to pronounce it. It's astonishing how many words are misunderstood simply because they are mispronounced. Words get mangled in surprisingly inventive ways. For example, people often switch letters and destroy nice little words that never did *them* any harm, such as, *abhor* (hate) becomes uh-BOR rather than ab-HOR.

One comedian has theorized that the number of consonants in English is constant. If a consonant is omitted in one place, it turns up in another. For example, when a Bostonian "pahks" his "cah," the lost r's migrate southwest, causing a Texan to "warsh" his car and invest in "erl wells."

People have also been known to drop letters. For instance, the food poisoning known as *salmonella* is correctly pronounced sal-muh-**NEL**-uh. Dropping the first *l* results in sam-uh-NEL-uh. (Sam 'n' Ella may be the speaker's close friends, but they are not the same as food poisoning).

The pronunciation problem is especially acute with words that can function as more than one part of speech. The word *ally* is a case in point. As a noun, it's pronounced AL-eye. As a verb, it's pronounced uh-LY.

In addition, people often insert an extra letter or two, which can make the word unrecognizable. For instance, *ambidextrous* (able to use either hand) has four syllables and is correctly pronounced am-bi-**DEK**-strus. But sometimes speakers add an extra syllable to get am-bi-**DEKS**-tree-us or am-bi-**DEKS**-tru-us.

Even the simple word *picture* can get warped as *pitcher*. As a result, no one knows what anyone else is talking about. Learning to say some words correctly is not always a piece of cake, but incorrect pronunciations can make it impossible to define the word.

The most effective way to learn how to pronounce new words is by using a dictionary. Get a reliable desk or pocket dictionary. It's the best source for the words you need to get you where you want to go. More on how to pick a dictionary later in this chapter.

## SEE AND SAY

How well do you pronounce commonplace words? Take the following self-test to see. Read the word and definition. Then pronounce each word. Answers follow.

| Word | Meaning | Pronunciation |
|---|---|---|
| 1. Amish | Pennsylvania Dutch | |
| 2. aplomb | assurance | |
| 3. awry | wrong, crooked | |
| 4. banquet | feast | |
| 5. buffet | self-service meal | |
| 6. buoy | floating marker | |
| 7. Celtic | Irish | |
| 8. denouement | conclusion | |
| 9. entrepreneur | businessperson | |
| 10. fracas | noisy fight | |
| 11. hegemony | leadership | |
| 12. insouciant | carefree | |
| 13. khaki | light brown | |
| 14. larynx | voice box | |
| 15. mausoleum | tomb | |
| 16. niche | corner | |
| 17. penchant | inclination | |

| Word | Meaning | Pronunciation |
|---|---|---|
| 18. posthumous | after death | |
| 19. quagmire | swamp | |
| 20. remuneration | payment | |
| 21. shallot | onion | |
| 22. toupee | hairpiece | |
| 23. vehement | fiery, passionate | |
| 24. verbiage | wordy | |
| 25. worsted | yarn | |

### ANSWERS

**Pronunciation**

1. AH-mish
2. uh-PLAHM
3. uh-RY
4. BAN-kwet
5. buh-FAY
6. BOO-ee
7. KEL-tik
8. day-noo-MAH
9. ahn-truh-pruh-NUR
10. FRAY-kis
11. hi-JE-muh-nee
12. in-SOO-see-int
13. KA-kee
14. LAR-ingks
15. maw-suh-LEE-um
16. NICH (rhymes with itch)
17. PEN-chint
18. PAHS-chu-mus
19. KWAG-myr
20. ri-myoo-nuh-RAY-shin
21. SHAL-it or shuh-LAHT
22. too-PAY
23. VEE-uh-mint
24. VUR-bee-ij
25. WUUS-tid

## GET CARDED: USE WORD CARDS

One of the most effective ways to make a word your own is through repetition. Going over the word can help you master its meaning as well as pronunciation and usage.

Try this idea: buy a stack of three by five index cards. As you read through the following chapters, write each difficult spelling word on the front of an index card, one word per card. Then write the definition on the back. Here's a sample:

matriarch

FRONT:

the female head of a family or tribe

BACK:

You can't win it if you're not in it, so try these three steps:

1. Study the cards every chance you get.
2. Take them with you on the bus, train, and plane; hide them in your lap and sneak a peek during dull meetings.
3. Rotate the order of the cards so you learn rather than just memorize.

## Kissing Cousins: Synonyms and Antonyms

*Synonyms* are words that are nearly the same in meaning. *Antonyms* are words that are opposites. Learning different synonyms and antonyms can help you swell your vocabulary and express yourself with greater clarity. Try it now.

Complete the following chart by writing at least one synonym and antonym for each word. Then see how many more synonyms and antonyms you can get through brainstorming. Possible answers follow.

WHILE WE'RE FOCUSING ON PRONUNCIATION, ONE OF THE TOUGHEST TONGUE TWISTERS IS: "THE SIXTH SICK SHEIK'S SIXTH SHEEP'S SICK." THEN THERE'S ALWAYS THIS ONE: "THE SINKING STEAMER SUNK."

| Word | Synonyms | Antonyms |
|---|---|---|
| adapt | | |
| authentic | | |
| chronic | | |
| conquer | | |
| frustrate | | |
| indulge | | |
| naive | | |
| punish | | |
| relinquish | | |
| sullen | | |

## POSSIBLE ANSWERS:

| Word | Synonyms | Antonyms |
|---|---|---|
| adapt | adjust, accustom, accommodate | disarrange, dislocate |
| authentic | genuine, real, legitimate | fake, counterfeit, bogus, imitation |
| chronic | habitual, ongoing, constant | one time, single |
| conquer | defeat, vanquish, overwhelm | surrender, yield, forfeit, give up |
| frustrate | baffle, beat, disappoint | facilitate, encourage |
| indulge | tolerate, humor, allow, permit | prohibit, deter, restrain, enjoin |
| naive | innocent, ingenuous | worldly, urbane, suave |
| punish | discipline, castigate | reward, compensate, remunerate |
| relinquish | quit, renounce | perpetuate, keep |
| sullen | irritable, morose, moody | cheerful, jolly, blithe, happy |

## WORKING UNDERCOVER: UNDERSTAND A WORD'S UNSTATED MEANINGS

Let's kick it up a notch by probing a word's *denotation* and *connotation*. Every word has a *denotation*—its dictionary meaning. In addition, some words have *connotations*—their understood meanings or emotional overtones. For example, both *house* and *home* have the same denotation—a shelter. *Home*, however, carries a connotation of warmth and love not present in *house*.

Slight differences in connotative meaning are important for precise speech and writing. For example, do you *adore*, *cherish*, *have affection for*, *worship*, *revere*, *treasure*, *esteem*, *honor*, or *prize* your significant other? All these words are synonyms for love, but there's a world of understood difference between saying "I love you" and saying "I honor you."

Let's take the opposite of love: *hate*. Do you *abhor*, *despise*, *scorn*, *abominate*, *curse*, *condemn*, *shun*, or *spurn* your most bitter foe? *Cursing* is not the same as *shunning* because the former involves foul words, while the latter is silent. Likewise, *scorning* is not nearly the same as *condemning*.

Test your understanding of connotation and denotation by completing the following chart. Write a plus sign (+) next to any word with a *positive* connotation or a dash (–) next to any word with a *negative* connotation.

When would you use each of these words? Why?

| Word | Connotation | |
|---|---|---|
| 1. emaciated | ____ (+ word) | ____(– word) |
| 2. slender | ____ (+ word) | ____(– word) |
| 3. cheap | ____ (+ word) | ____(– word) |
| 4. thrifty | ____ (+ word) | ____(– word) |
| 5. stubborn | ____ (+ word) | ____(– word) |
| 6. steadfast | ____ (+ word) | ____(– word) |
| 7. reckless | ____ (+ word) | ____(– word) |
| 8. bold | ____ (+ word) | ____(– word) |
| 9. obstinate | ____ (+ word) | ____(– word) |
| 10. constant | ____ (+ word) | ____(– word) |

### ANSWERS

All the even-numbered choices have a positive connotation; all the odd-numbered choices have a negative connotation—even though the word pairs have basically the same denotations.

## INTERMISSION TIME

Take a stretch by completing this easy quiz. Just match each of the vocabulary words with its definition. Then write the letter of the definition in the space provided next to each word. Make a word card for each word you get wrong.

DOING WORD PUZZLES AND GAMES, EVERYTHING FROM CROSSWORD PUZZLES TO SCRABBLE®, CAN ALSO HELP YOU INCREASE YOUR VOCABULARY.

| | |
|---|---|
| _____1. inalienable | a. mistakes |
| _____2. crotchety | b. academic |
| _____3. lumbering | c. thinking |
| _____4. hinterlands | d. not to be taken away |
| _____5. endemic | e. grind |
| _____6. kiosk | f. to give in |
| _____7. distraught | g. left unplanted |
| _____8. macerate | h. moving in a clumsy way |
| _____9. cognition | i. sober, self-restraining |
| _____10. abstemious | j. greatly upset |
| _____11. didactic | k. grouchy |
| _____12. capitulate | l. common in a particular area |
| _____13. decadence | m. decline |
| _____14. winsome | n. great many |
| _____15. turbid | o. lacking firmness |
| _____16. myriad | p. region remote from cities |
| _____17. loath | q. murky |
| _____18. fallow | r. unwilling |
| _____19. errata | s. magazine stand |
| _____20. flaccid | t. charming |

ABOUT 80 PERCENT OF THE WORLD'S COMPUTER TEXT IS WRITTEN IN ENGLISH.

### ANSWERS

| | | | |
|---|---|---|---|
| 1. d | 6. s | 11. b | 16. n |
| 2. k | 7. j | 12. f | 17. r |
| 3. h | 8. e | 13. m | 18. g |
| 4. p | 9. c | 14. t | 19. a |
| 5. l | 10. i | 15. q | 20. o |

## BREAK DANCE: BREAK A WORD INTO SMALLER PARTS THAT YOU CAN DECODE EASILY

A surprisingly large number of words can be divided into parts that you can figure out easily. If you can define the parts, then you can often decode the entire word. There are three main word parts to know: *prefixes*, *suffixes*, and *roots*.

- A *prefix* is a letter or a group of letters placed at the beginning of a word to change its meaning.

- A *suffix* is a letter or a group of letters placed at the end of a word to change its meaning.
- A *root* is a base or stem form of many words.

For example, if you know the Latin root *ami* means "like" or "love," you can easily figure out that *amiable* means "pleasant and friendly." Similarly, you could deduce that a*morous* means "loving." Even if you can't define a word exactly, recognizing the root will still give you a general idea of the word's meaning.

Knowing prefixes, suffixes, and roots is such an important way to expand your vocabulary that three full chapters—Chapters 2, 3, and 4—focus on teaching you these techniques.

## YOU CAN LOOK IT UP: USE A PRINT DICTIONARY AND AN ON-LINE THESAURUS

I know, I know, looking up a word is a pain. So is exercise, but they both work. Using a dictionary will help you check what a word means and how it is used.

Actually, dictionaries give us a lot more than a list of words and their meanings. Think of a dictionary as a good friend. There are two main kinds of dictionaries: abridged and unabridged.

- An *unabridged* dictionary is complete. The *Oxford English Dictionary (OED)* is the standard unabridged dictionary. It contains more than 500,000 entries. Don't rush right out to buy one to stash in your briefcase, however; it attempts to record the birth and history of every printed word in the language since about A.D. 1050 to the current date of publication. The *OED* now contains about 60 million words in 20 volumes.

- An *abridged* dictionary is shortened. It is fine for everyday purposes, like looking up words, propping open doors, and pressing prom flowers. You'll want an unabridged dictionary if you're interested in knowing everything there is to know about a word.

> PRINT DICTIONARIES DON'T RUN OUT OF BATTERIES; HANDHELD COMPUTERIZED DICTIONARIES ARE LIGHT AND EASY TO CARRY. IT'S YOUR CALL. JUST BE SURE TO USE A DICTIONARY WHEN YOU CAN.

To make your shopping trip easier, here are five of the standard abridged dictionaries you may wish to consider. Compare them to see which one best suits your needs.

1. *Webster's New World Dictionary of the American Language*
2. *Webster's New Collegiate Dictionary (latest edition)*
3. *The American Heritage Dictionary*
4. *The Concise Oxford Dictionary of Current English*
5. *The Random House College Dictionary*

A built-in computer thesaurus program provides synonyms and antonyms for almost any word you highlight. These programs come as part of any standard word-processing package.

> IF YOU FIND THAT YOUR JOB OR LIFESTYLE REQUIRES YOU TO DEFINE REGIONAL AND FOREIGN TERMS, YOU MAY WISH TO CONSULT THE **DICTIONARY OF AMERICAN REGIONAL ENGLISH**, THE **DICTIONARY OF FOREIGN PHRASES AND ABBREVIATIONS**, THE **DICTIONARY OF FOREIGN TERMS**, OR **THE HARPER DICTIONARY OF FOREIGN TERMS.**

These thesaurus programs are especially useful for distinguishing among homonyms. If you intended to type "weather" but instead keyboarded "whether," the thesaurus will give you synonyms for *atmospheric conditions*, *climate*, *meteorology*, and *the elements*. This can help you keep your homonyms straight. More on this in Chapter 6.

## Games People Play: Create Mnemonics (Memory Tricks) to Help You Differentiate Confusing Words

*Mnemonics* (pronounced ne-MOHN-iks) are memory games that help you remember everything from the order of the planets to your grocery list. Mnemonics are another technique to help you distinguish between easily confused words. For example, to remember that *principal* means "main" (as in the principal of a school), look at the last three letters: the princi***pal*** is your ***pal***. To remember that *principle* means "rule," remember that both words end in ***le***.

Likewise, *stationary* means standing still (both words contain an *a*) while *stationery* is for letters (both words have an *er*). *Desert* and *dessert* become easier to define when you remember that dessert has a double *s*, like "strawberry shortcake."

You might ask, "Why not just look the word up in the dictionary and be done with it?" No doubt that looking up a word in the dictionary is the best way to check its meaning, but let's get real. Everyone knows that saving for a rainy day, and looking both ways before crossing the street are also solid pieces of advice, but how often do we follow them? Besides, you might not always have a dictionary handy. So why not create your own mnemonics to help you remember the easily confused words that you use every day? There's more on this in Chapter 6.

> YOU CAN CREATE YOUR OWN ON-LINE DICTIONARY BY ADDING WORDS TO YOUR SPELL CHECKER. ONE TIME-SAVING TRICK IS TO ADD ALL THE PROPER NOUNS YOU REGULARLY USE.

## GETTING THE GIST: USE CONTEXT CLUES

When you read, you may come upon unfamiliar words. You can get clues to the meaning of unfamiliar words by the information surrounding the words, the *context*. To figure out the meaning of the unfamiliar word, you make inferences based on what you already know and the details that you are given in the sentence or paragraph. Here's an example:

> Just before midnight on April 14, 1912, one of the most dramatic and famous of all *maritime* disasters occurred, the sinking of the *Titanic*. The *Titanic* was the most luxurious ship afloat at the time, with its beautifully decorated staterooms, glittering crystal chandeliers, and elaborate food service.

How can you figure out that *maritime* must mean "related to the sea, nautical"? Use context clues:

**What you already know:** The *Titanic* was an oceanliner.
**Sentence details:** "The *Titanic* was the most luxurious ship afloat . . ."

Define *futile* as it is used in this passage:

> The "unsinkable" *Titanic* vanished under the water at 2:20 A.M., April 15. There were about 2,200 passengers aboard, and all but 678 died. The tragedy

was made even worse by the crew's futile rescue attempts. Since there were not enough lifeboats, hundreds of people died who could have survived.

I explain context clues in detail in Chapter 5.

## TALL TALES: LEARN WORD HISTORIES

In the 1600s, people believed that toads were poisonous, and that anyone who mistakenly ate a toad's leg instead of a frog's leg would die. Rather than swearing off frog's legs, people sought a cure for the "fatal" food poisoning. Performing in public, quack healers would sometimes hire an accomplice who would pretend to eat a toad, at which point his employer would whip out an instant remedy and "save" his helper's life. For his duties, the helper came to be called a "toad-eater." Since anyone who would consume anything as disgusting as a toad must be completely under his master's thumb, "toad-eater" or "toady" became the term for a bootlicking, fawning flatterer.

And that's how the term *toady* came to be.

English is a living language. From its Germanic beginnings, English absorbed influences from a wide variety of sources, including classical Greek and Latin to Italian, French, Spanish, and the Arabic states. English continues to absorb new words as our culture changes. In addition, a significant part of our vocabulary is artificially created to meet new situations. Exploring the history of these words, their *etymology*, can help you learn many useful everyday words. You'll learn loads of word histories in Chapter 8.

## USE IT OR LOSE IT: USE NEWLY LEARNED WORDS IN YOUR CONVERSATION AND WRITING

"Use it or lose it" applies to many fields, but especially to retaining the new words that you've learned. Using a word often in conversation and writing (when it fits, of course) will help you make it part of your everyday vocabulary.

In the chapters that follow, you'll practice what you've learned here, in addition to learning other ways to improve your everyday vocabulary.

MAKE SURE YOU HAVE THE WORD YOU WANT— BEFORE YOU EVEN WORRY ABOUT USING IT IN SPEECH AND WRITING.

# CHAPTER 2

# FRONT LOADING:

## LEARN PREFIXES

YOU MUST REMEMBER THIS

A prefix is a letter or group of letters placed at the beginning of a word to change its meaning.

ALL THE RIGHT MOVES

Knowing prefixes can help you figure out the meaning of many everyday words that you hear and read.

"How can we *circumvent* this traffic jam?" the driver of your carpool growls as traffic comes to a grinding halt. If you've never heard the word *circumvent* before, you might have to scramble for an answer. But by the end of this chapter you'll know a secret shortcut to this answer. Prefixes! When you learn your prefixes, you can say to yourself: Let's see, *circum-* is a prefix that means "around." Therefore, *circumvent* means to "go around." Then you can tell your buddy to try the side road—assuming your sense of direction is as good as your vocabulary.

A prefix is a letter or a group of letters placed at the beginning of a word to affect its meaning. Knowing common prefixes is a *very* useful skill because it enables you to figure out the meaning of many unfamiliar words. In addition, by studying prefixes as the building blocks of words, you can easily master thousands of English words. In this chapter, you'll learn all about prefixes and how they can help you improve your everyday vocabulary.

## TEST YOURSELF

How much do you know about prefixes? Find out with the simple exercise below. Each of the following words starts with a prefix. Use what you already know about prefixes to see how many of these words you can define. Select the letter of the correct meaning for each of the following **boldfaced** words.

1. **accede**

| a. go very fast | b. agree | c. excessive | d. debate |
|---|---|---|---|

2. **hypocrisy**

| a. overpriced | b. false virtue | c. sweet natured | d. injection |
|---|---|---|---|

3. **subsistence**

| a. wealth | b. existence | c. under water | d. farming |
|---|---|---|---|

4. **aggregate**

| a. complete | b. annoy | c. marbles | d. clot |
|---|---|---|---|

5. **ultramarine**

| a. fashionable | b. weird | c. deep blue | d. famous |
|---|---|---|---|

6. **hyperactivity**

| a. illness | b. medicine | c. excessive activity | d. low |
|---|---|---|---|

7. **catacomb**

| a. comb for cats | b. dessert | c. underground room | d. crooked |
|---|---|---|---|

8. **amoral**

| a. very moral | b. not moral | c. story lesson | d. high spirits |
|---|---|---|---|

9. **compress**

| a. squeeze | b. heal | c. measurement tool | d. pat |
|---|---|---|---|

10. **supercilious**

| a. arrogant | b. high achieving | c. very silly | d. long hairs |
|---|---|---|---|

## ANSWERS

| | |
|---|---|
| 1. b. agree | 6. c. excessive activity |
| 2. b. false virtue | 7. c. underground room |
| 3. b. existence | 8. b. not moral |
| 4. a. complete | 9. a. squeeze |
| 5. c. deep blue | 10. a. arrogant |

The following chart shows one way you might have used prefixes to figure out the meanings of these words.

| **Word** | **Prefix** | **Prefix Meaning** | **Word Meaning** |
|---|---|---|---|
| accede | ac- | to, toward | agree |
| hypocrisy | hypo- | under, below | false virtue |
| subsistence | sub- | under | existence |
| aggregate | ag- | do, act | complete |
| ultramarine | ultra- | beyond | deep blue |
| hyperactivity | hyper- | excessive | excessive activity |
| catacomb | cat- | down | underground room |
| amoral | a- | not | not moral |
| compress | com- | with | squeeze |
| supercilious | super- | over, beyond | arrogant |

Following are the key prefixes that will help you unlock the meaning of many useful everyday words.

## IT'S GREEK TO ME: GREEK PREFIXES

The Greeks have given us some helpful prefixes. Knowing these cute little bits and pieces of words opens up a whole new world of definition. Here are ten prefixes to get you started.

| **Prefix** | **Meaning** | **Examples** | **Definition** |
|---|---|---|---|
| a- | not, without | atypical | not typical |
| anthro- | man | anthropology | study of man |
| anti- | against | antipathy | hatred |
| aster-, astro- | star | asteroid | star-like body |

| Prefix | Meaning | Examples | Definition |
|---|---|---|---|
| auto- | self | automobile | self-moving |
| biblio- | book | bibliophile | book lover |
| bio- | life | biography | person's life story |
| chrom- | color | polychromatic | many-colored |
| chron- | time | chronological | time order |
| cosmo- | world | cosmopolitan | worldly |

## WIN ONE FOR THE GIPPER

Take a break and test yourself by completing the following chart. For each word, first write the prefix and its meaning. Then use what you learned about prefixes to define each word. Since all's fair in love, war, and mastering vocabulary, feel free to look back at the ten prefixes you just learned.

| Word | Prefix | Meaning | Word Meaning |
|---|---|---|---|
| 1. asterisk | | | |
| 2. synchronize | | | |
| 3. autonomy | | | |
| 4. anthropoid | | | |
| 5. anemia | | | |
| 6. automaton | | | |
| 7. antidote | | | |
| 8. biodegradable | | | |
| 9. bibliophile | | | |
| 10. astronaut | | | |

SOME OF THESE PREFIXES CAN ALSO FUNCTION AS ROOTS, DEPENDING ON THEIR PLACEMENT IN THE WORD.

## ANSWERS

| Word | Prefix | Meaning | Word Meaning |
|---|---|---|---|
| 1. asterisk | aster- | star | star-shaped mark |
| 2. synchronize | chron- | time | agree in time |
| 3. autonomy | auto- | self | self-government |
| 4. anthropoid | anthro- | human | resembling human |
| 5. anemia | a- | not | blood deficiency |
| 6. automaton | auto- | self | robot |
| 7. antidote | anti- | against | remedy against poison |
| 8. biodegradable | bio- | life | decays and is absorbed into the environment |
| 9. bibliophile | biblio- | books | lover of books |
| 10. astronaut | astro-, aster- | star | "star sailor" |

Below are ten more prefixes that have made their way from ancient Greece to contemporary America. Read through the prefixes, meanings, and examples. Pause after each row to see how many other words you can think of that start with or contain the same prefix.

| Prefix | Meaning | Examples | Definition |
|---|---|---|---|
| dem- | people | democracy | government by the people |
| eu- | good | eulogize | speak well of someone |
| gee-, geo- | earth | geography | writing about earth |
| graph-, gram- | write | grapheme | unit of a writing system |
| hydra-, hydro- | water | hydrophobia | fear of water |
| hyper- | over | hypercritical | overly critical |
| hypo | under | hypodermic | under the skin |
| micro- | small | microscope | tool for looking at small objects |
| mis- | hate | misanthropy | hatred of people |
| mono- | one | monotone | one tone |

## GO TO THE HEAD OF THE WORD

You know the drill: Identify the prefix, define it, and then define the word. Refer to the previous chart if you need a quick review.

| Word | Prefix | Meaning | Word Meaning |
|---|---|---|---|
| 1. geocentric | | | |
| 2. demography | | | |
| 3. demagogue | | | |
| 4. euphemism | | | |
| 5. euphonious | | | |
| 6. euphoria | | | |
| 7. geology | | | |
| 8. graphic | | | |
| 9. microfilm | | | |
| 10. monotheism | | | |

## ANSWERS

| Word | Prefix | Meaning | Word Meaning |
|---|---|---|---|
| 1. geocentric | geo- | earth | having or relating to the earth as center |
| 2. demography | dem- | people | statistical study of human populations |
| 3. demagogue | dem- | people | rabble-rouser |
| 4. euphemism | eu- | good | substitution of a mild expression for one that may offend |
| 5. euphonious | eu- | good | pleasing sound |
| 6. euphoria | eu- | good | intense feeling of well-being |
| 7. geology | geo- | earth | study of the earth |
| 8. graphic | graph- | write | written |
| 9. microfilm | micro- | small | small film |
| 10. monotheism | mono- | one | belief in one God |

Humorist Joe Bob Briggs says the Spanish word *estacionamiento* is his favorite word. He learned to pronounce it with just the right roll before he found out what it means: parking lot.

Since you're on a roll, too, how about ten more Greek-based prefixes? How many of these have you heard in your daily conversation?

| Prefix | Meaning | Examples | Definition |
|---|---|---|---|
| pan- | all | panacea | cure-all |
| peri- | around | perimeter | outer measurement |
| phil- | love | philanthropy | love of humanity |
| phob- | fear | claustrophobia | fear of confined spaces |
| poly- | many | polyphonic | having many sounds |
| pseudo- | false | pseudoscience | false science |
| psycho- | mind | psychology | study of the mind |
| syn-, sym- | together | synthesis | putting together |
| tele- | distance | telephone | phone |
| theo- | God | theology | study of God or religion |

## Prefix Party

"Once more unto the breach, dear friends." Identify the prefix, define it, and then define the word. I promise I won't tattle if you look back at what you have already learned.

| Word | Prefix | Meaning | Word Meaning |
|---|---|---|---|
| 1. Pan-American | | | |
| 2. pandemic | | | |
| 3. polygon | | | |
| 4. polynomial | | | |
| 5. polyglot | | | |
| 6. symbiosis | | | |
| 7. symmetrical | | | |
| 8. synopsis | | | |
| 9. telecommunication | | | |
| 10. telepathy | | | |

## ANSWERS

| Word | Prefix | Meaning | Word Meaning |
|---|---|---|---|
| 1. Pan-American | pan- | all | all of the Americas |
| 2. pandemic | pan- | all | widespread disease |
| 3. polygon | poly- | many | figure with many sides |
| 4. polyglot | poly- | many | knowing many languages |
| 5. polynomial | poly- | many | a math expression having two or more terms |
| 6. symbiosis | sym- | together | two dissimilar organisms living together |
| 7. symmetrical | sym- | together | identical corresponding parts |
| 8. synopsis | syn- | together | summary |
| 9. telecommunication | tele- | distance | communication across distances |
| 10. telepathy | tele- | distance | transference of thought |

## LATIN (WORD) LOVERS: LATIN PREFIXES AND ROOTS

Not to be outdone by Greek, Latin has given us some extremely useful prefixes and roots. The Latin prefix *circum-* is a case in point. *Circum-*, which means "around," can be used to form heaps of useful everyday words. Here are twelve such examples:

| Word | Definition |
|---|---|
| circumambulate | to walk around |
| circumference | the outer boundary of something |
| circumfluent | flowing around |
| circumfuse | to pour or spread |
| circumlocution | a roundabout way of speaking |
| circumnavigate | to sail around |
| circumpolar | around the North or South Pole |
| circumrotate | to rotate like a wheel |
| circumscribe | to enclose |
| circumspect | cautious, prudent |
| circumvent | to surround or encompass |

WAY BEFORE ENGLISH WAS THE COMMON TONGUE, LATIN WAS USED AROUND THE WORLD IN POLITICS, LITERATURE, AND SCIENCE. AS A RESULT, MANY WORDS WE STILL USE COME FROM LATIN.

And that's just the beginning. Check out these ten Latin prefixes and roots, their meanings, and examples.

| Prefix | Meaning | Examples |
|---|---|---|
| 1. a- | to, in, at | ascribe |
| 2. act-, | do, act | action |
| 3. ad-, ag- | to, toward | adsorb, aggradation |
| 4. ante- | before | anteroom |
| 5. bene- | good | beneficial |
| 6. bi- | two | bicycle |
| 7. capt-, cept- | take | captain |
| 6. ceed-, cess- | go | proceeding, process |
| 7. clud-, clus- | close | exclude, inclusion |
| 8. co-, com-, con-, col- | with, together | coworker, commune, conduct, collaborate |
| 9. contra- | against, opposite | contraband |
| 10. cur- | run | current |

## HEADS UP!

Use what you've learned so far about Latin prefixes to figure out the meanings of the following ten words. Write the letter of your choice in the space provided.

_____ 1. cursive
a. flowing handwriting c. cruel
b. foul language d. commonplace

_____ 2. agitate
a. clean c. tranquilize
b. tap your foot d. stir up

_____ 3. adjoin
a. separate c. attach
b. listen closely d. disunite

_____ 4. cosigner
a. underwriter c. sign language specialist
b. dependent d. joint signer

_____ 5. concede
a. yield c. augment
b. build d. curtail

> OTHER WORDS THAT HAVE BEEN FORMED WITH THE LATIN PREFIX **CONTRA-**, INCLUDE, **CONTRADICT** (SPEAK AGAINST), **CONTRAINDICATE** (TO GO AGAINST INDICATIONS), AND **CONTRARY** (OPPOSED IN NATURE).

_____ 6. depress

a. elevate
b. bring down
c. upraise
d. invigorate

_____ 7. adjudicate

a. subjoin
b. deduct
c. lessen
d. mediate

_____ 8. affix

a. withhold
b. repair
c. to fasten
d. injure

_____ 9. confederation

a. Southerners
b. antagonism
c. alliance
d. aversion

_____ 10. collateral

a. bond
b. far away
c. considerably
d. dependent

WINSTON CHURCHILL ONCE SAID, "OLD WORDS ARE BEST, AND SHORT WORDS ARE BEST OF ALL."

### ANSWERS

1. a
2. d
3. c
4. d
5. a
6. b
7. d
8. c
9. c
10. a

Learn ten more Latin prefixes to help you figure out which words could become *your* new favorites.

| Prefix | Meaning | Examples | Definition |
|---|---|---|---|
| 1. de- | down | demolish | tear down |
| 2. e- | out | elongate | stretch out |
| 3. ex- | out | exterior | outside |
| 4. inter- | between | intercom | two-way radio |
| 5. infra- | under | infrared | rays under red |
| 6. mal- | bad | malodor | bad odor |
| 7. male- | evil | maledict | cursed |
| 8. ob- | toward | obedient | dutiful |
| 9. per- | through | perambulate | walk through |
| 10. post- | after | postpone | do after |

## MIX 'N MATCH

Now apply what you read to figuring out the following ten words. Each one uses a prefix you just learned. Choose the best definition; you will have definitions left over.

1. __ excavate
2. __ infrasonic
3. __ impart
4. __ maladroit
5. __ malefactor
6. __ eccentric
7. __ impatient
8. __ effluent
9. __ inscribe
10. __ indecent

a. flowing forth
b. criminal
c. vulgar
d. write on
e. teach
f. attractive
g. restless
h. dig out
i. awkward
j. odd
k. comely
l. invocation
m. sound waves with a frequency below the audible range

### ANSWERS

1. h
2. m
3. e
4. i
5. b
6. j
7. g
8. a
9. d
10. c

## MAKE UP YOUR MIND!

Some prefixes have more than one meaning. Here are some examples of Latin prefixes that serve the same double duty.

| Prefix | Meaning | Examples |
|---|---|---|
| il- | in, into | illuminate |
| il- | not | illiterate |
| im- | in, into | import |
| im- | not | immodest |
| in- | in, into | inhabit |
| in- | not | inflexible |
| ir- | in, into | irradiate |
| ir- | not | irregular |

THE PREFIX **PRE-** MEANS "BEFORE" AS IN **PREMATURE; PRO-** MEANS "FORWARD," AS IN **PROCLAIM.**

THE PREFIX **SUB-** MEANS "UNDER," AS IN **SUBMARINE, SUPER-** MEANS "OVER," AS IN **SUPERIOR,** AND **TRANS-** MEANS "ACROSS, OVER," AS IN **TRANSCEND.**

Based on the meaning of its prefix, define each of the following words:

1. accord
2. irradiate
3. predestination
4. reincarnation
5. convolute
6. invoke
7. irrelevant
8. excommunicate

## ANSWERS

1. agree
2. illuminate
3. fate
4. rebirth
5. twist up
6. request
7. not pertinent
8. expel from communion with church

## YOU CAN COUNT ON THIS!

The symbols we use for numbers (1, 2, 3, 4, etc.) come from the Arabs—the first great mathematicians. The words we use to speak or write these symbols (one, two, three, four, etc.) are from the Anglo-Saxons.

How many sides does the Pentagon have? How many tentacles does an octopus have? If you know your number prefixes, these questions are a snap to answer. The envelope, please: The Pentagon has five sides (*penta-* = five); an octopus has eight tentacles (*octo-* = eight).

As you can see, when we want to combine a number and a word to form another word, such as a synonym for a "five-sided figure," we use the Greek or Roman word as a prefix indicating the number.

Here are ten Greek and Latin prefixes that show the numbers one to ten.

| Number | Prefix | Example |
|---|---|---|
| 1 | uni- | unicycle |
| 2 | bi- | bicycle |
| 3 | tri- | tripod |
| 4 | quad- | quadrangle |

| Number | Prefix | Example |
|---|---|---|
| 5 | penta- | pentameter |
| 6 | hexa- | hexagon |
| 7 | hepta- | Heptateuch |
| 8 | oct- | octet |
| 9 | nov- | novena |
| 10 | deca- | Decalogue |

> THE 100 MOST COMMONLY USED WORDS IN ENGLISH ALL COME FROM THE ANGLO-SAXONS.

## TRAVELIN' LITE: ANGLO-SAXON PREFIXES

Below are the five most common Anglo-Saxon prefixes and their variations. Read through the chart and examples. To help you remember the prefixes, complete the self-test that follows:

| Prefix | Meaning | Examples | Definition |
|---|---|---|---|
| 1. a- | on, to, at, by | ablaze | on fire |
| 2. be- | around, over | besiege | attack |
| 3. mis- | wrong, badly | mistake | error |
| 4. over- | above, beyond | overreach | reach too high |
| 5. un- | not | unwilling | not willing |

## WORDS IN CONTEXT

Define each of the following underlined words based on the way it is used in the phrase. Write the letter of your choice in the space provided.

_____ 1. miscarriage of justice
a. villain c. example
b. detail d. failure

_____ 2. beseech emotionally
a. implore c. shriek
b. deny d. pursue

_____ 3. something strange is afoot
a. underneath c. clandestine
b. going on d. covert

_____ 4. unethical behavior
a. judicial c. unprincipled
b. impartial d. competent

_____ 5. an overwrought child
a. heavy c. placid
b. unmannerly d. excited

### ANSWERS

1. d
2. a
3. b
4. c
5. d

# CHAPTER 3

# GET TO THE ROOT OF THE MATTER: LEARN ROOTS

> YOU MUST REMEMBER THIS
>
> A root is a stem or base form for many words.
>
> ALL THE RIGHT MOVES
>
> Roots are the building blocks of words. Knowing even a handful of roots can help you decode many, many words.

***After interviewing a particularly laconic job candidate, the interviewer described the person to her boss as rather monosyllabic. Her boss said, "Really? Where is Monosyllabia?"***

***Thinking that he was just kidding, she played along and said that it was just south of Elbonia. He replied, "Oh, you mean over by Croatia?"***

In Chapter 2, you learned that prefixes can help you decode many words. As a result, you'd never get tricked by the word *monosyllabic*, because you know that *mono-* means "one." In this chapter, you'll dig into many useful word roots. Then you'll know that *syllable* means "a sound group." *Monosyllable*, then, must mean "one syllable."

Whenever you come upon an unfamiliar word, first check to see if it has a recognizable root. For example, remembering that the Greek root *geo* means "earth" would help you define geology as "the history of the earth." Even if you can't define a word exactly, recognizing the root will still give you a general idea of the word's meaning. For instance, if you see *geocentric*, you might not know its exact meaning, but knowing the root *geo* would help you figure out that *geocentric* has to do with the center of the earth or earth as the center.

Following are some common word roots that can help you figure out the meaning of many words that you'll come upon in your daily speech and writing.

## TEST YOURSELF

How good are you at using roots to decipher words? Each word below contains a root. Use what you already know about roots to see how many of these words you can decode. Select the correct meaning for each of the following **boldfaced** words. Write the letter of your choice in the space provided.

____1. **thermostat**
a. ruler
b. judicial procedure
c. device that maintains temperature
d. device that measures speed

____2. **genetics**
a. science of heredity
b. article of clothing
c. cloning
d. legislation

____3. **androgynous**
a. lenient
b. strongly resembling
c. false
d. neither specifically feminine nor masculine

____4. **biped**
a. pipe
b. horse
c. mythical creature
d. two-footed animal

____5. **millennium**
a. 100 years
b. 1,000 years
c. 10,000 years
d. 100,000 years

____6. **archenemy**
a. chief enemy
b. weakest foe
c. benefactor
d. angel

_____7. **dictum**

a. instruct
b. ordain
c. saying or maxim
d. stomach lining

_____8. **putrefaction**

a. storage method
b. freezing
c. eating raw flesh
d. rotting

_____9. **oligarchy**

a. obliging
b. rule by many
c. rule by a few people
d. commonwealth

_____10. **annuity**

a. windfall
b. stock fund
c. income paid every year
d. income paid monthly

THE DEPTH AND PRECISION OF ENGLISH HAVE HELPED MAKE IT THE FOREMOST LANGUAGE OF SCIENCE, DIPLOMACY, AND INTERNATIONAL BUSINESS—AND THE MEDIUM OF T-SHIRTS FROM TIJUANA TO TIMBUKTU.

### ANSWERS

| | |
|---|---|
| 1. c | 6. a |
| 2. a | 7. c |
| 3. d | 8. d |
| 4. d | 9. c |
| 5. b | 10. c |

## ROOT RULES

So we're all reading from the same page, here are the basic guidelines for using word roots:

1. A word can contain more than one root.

   **Example:** *Matrilineal* contains the roots *matra* and *lineal.* Since
   *matra* means "mother" and
   *lineal* means "line,"
   *matrilineal* means "determining descent through the female line."

2. Some roots form whole words by themselves.

   **Examples:** *Pater* means "father." *Term* means "end."

3. Some roots must be combined with other word elements to form words.
   **Examples:** *prim* (first) + al = *primal* (first)
   *sequ* (follow) + el = *sequel* (something following)

4. Prefixes and suffixes are often added to roots to alter the word's meaning.
   **Example:** *Harmonic* means "music." *Philharmonic* means "love of music."

5. Some roots can also function as prefixes, depending on their placement in a word.
   **Example:** *Graphy* means "writing"
   Used as a root, it becomes *calligraphy*.
   Used as a prefix, it becomes *graphology*.

## GREEK ROOTS

Grouping roots by common themes and concerns can make them much easier to learn. Let's start with the ancient Greeks. *Splish*, *splash*, let's take a bath with the Greek root for water—*hydro*.

## THE WATER'S FINE, SO DIVE RIGHT IN

According to Greek mythology, the ancients were menaced by a hideous nine-headed serpent with breath so bad it could knock you deader than a doornail. Killing this monster was no easy matter. When you sliced off one head, two grew in its place. Unfortunately for those being menaced, the central head was immortal. Since the ancient Greeks didn't have the Ghostbusters, they sent Hercules in to dispatch this many-headed menace. Herc was triumphant when he burned off the eight peripheral heads and buried the ninth under a huge rock. The monster that Herc destroyed took its name from its home in a watery marsh: *Hydra*, from the Greek root *hydr(o)*, meaning "water."

Quite a few useful words are formed from the "hydr" or "hydro" root. See how many of these "water words" you can figure out by matching them with the correct lettered definition:

| | |
|---|---|
| 1. hydrostat | a. power generated from water |
| 2. dehydrate | b. flower that needs much water |
| 3. hydrophobia | c. water on Earth |
| 4. hydroplane | d. rabies; literally, fear of water |

5. hydroponics — e. combine with water
6. hydropower — f. dry out
7. hydrate — g. water therapy
8. hydrangea — h. boat that travels on water
9. hydrotherapy — i. growing plants in water
10. hydrosphere — j. electrical device for detecting water

**ANSWERS**

| | |
|---|---|
| 1. j | 6. a |
| 2. f | 7. e |
| 3. d | 8. b |
| 4. h | 9. g |
| 5. i | 10. c |

## AU NATUREL

While we're on water, here are some Greek roots and words formed from them that concern the natural world.

| Root | Meaning | Example | Definition |
|---|---|---|---|
| andr | man | androgen | male hormone |
| gen | race | genetic | pertaining to genes |
| gyn | women | gynecologist | doctor for women |
| helio | sun | heliotrope | type of flower |
| ichthy | fish | ichthyology | study of fish |
| ornith | bird | ornithology | study of birds |
| polit | citizen | cosmopolitan | worldly |
| pyro | fire | pyrogenic | producing heat |
| thermo | heat | thermostat | device for regulating temperature |
| zoo | animal | zoology | study of animals |

## ROOT! ROOT! ROOT!

Assess what you've learned so far by completing the following chart. For each word, first write the root and its meaning. Then use what you've learned about roots to define each word. Don't hesitate to look back at what you just learned or to use a dictionary if you would like to.

| Word | Root | Meaning | Word Meaning |
|---|---|---|---|
| 1. android | | | |
| 2. engender | | | |
| 3. gene | | | |
| 4. gynarchy | | | |
| 5. heliocentric | | | |
| 6. ichthyoid | | | |
| 7. politician | | | |
| 8. polity | | | |
| 9. pyrography | | | |
| 10. pyrotechnics | | | |
| 11. ornithopod | | | |
| 12. thermodynamics | | | |
| 13. thermometer | | | |
| 14. zoological | | | |
| 15. zoometry | | | |

## ANSWERS

| Word | Root | Meaning | Word Meaning |
|---|---|---|---|
| 1. android | andr | man | man-shaped robot |
| 2. engender | gen | race | to produce |
| 3. gene | gen | race | unit of heredity |
| 4. gynarchy | gyn | women | government by women |
| 5. heliocentric | helio | sun | sun-centric |
| 6. ichthyoid | ichthy | fish | fishlike |
| 7. politician | polit | citizen | officeholder |
| 8. polity | polit | citizen | form of government |
| 9. pyrography | pyro | fire | burning designs on wood, etc. |
| 10. pyrotechnics | pyr | fire | fireworks |
| 11. ornithopod | ornith | bird | birdlike dinosaur |
| 12. thermodynamics | thermo | heat | using heat |
| 13. thermometer | thermo | heat | device for measuring temperature |
| 14. zoological | zoo | animal | about animals |
| 15. zoometry | zoo | animal | measuring animals |

## BODY TALK

*Soma* is the Greek root for "body." Let me hear your body talk with these roots and their meanings.

| Root | Meaning | Example |
|---|---|---|
| arteri | artery | artery |
| arthr | joint | arthritis |
| bronch | lung | bronchitis |
| cardio | heart | cardiovascular |
| chiro | hand | chiropractic |
| cranio | skull | cranium |
| derm | skin | dermatology |
| digit | finger, toe | digital |
| gastr | stomach | gastrology |
| hem | blood | hematology |
| laryn | larynx | larynx |
| neur | nerve | neurology |
| odont | tooth | orthodontist |
| ophthalm | eye | ophthalmology |
| oste | bone | osteopath |
| pneum | lung | pneumonia |
| pulmo | lung | pulmonary |
| sacr | flesh | sacrament |

FROM THE GREEK AND LATIN ROOT **GNO** ("TO KNOW") COMES SUCH WORDS AS **COGNIZANT** (AWARE), **INCOGNITO** (DISGUISED), **DIAGNOSTICIAN** (AN EXPERT IN DIAGNOSING ILLNESS), AND **COGNITION** (PERCEPTION).

## YOU CAN GET THERE FROM HERE

If you're like me, you often have to measure something. And if you're *really* like me, you never have the yardstick or tape measure, so most of your measurements are rather—um—casual. To make sure that you understand the units of measurement, here are some common Greek roots concerned with distances, units, and age.

| Root | Meaning | Example | Definition |
|---|---|---|---|
| acr | top | acrophobia | fear of high places |
| arch | first | archbishop | highest bishop |
| ger | old | geriatric | relating to old age |
| horo | hour | hologe | time piece |
| macro, mega | large | megalomania | delusions of greatness |
| meter | measure | altimeter | device to measure altitude |

| Root | Meaning | Example | Definition |
|---|---|---|---|
| pan | all | panhuman | for all humanity |
| ped | foot | pedometer | device for measuring steps |

## LATIN ROOTS

If you think we've borrowed a lot of roots from the Greeks, wait until you see what we've recycled from Latin. For example, the Latin root *nomin, nomen* ("name") has given us a great many words, including this half dozen:

| Word | Meaning |
|---|---|
| ignominious | disgracing one's name |
| misnomer | wrong name |
| nomenclature | system of naming |
| nominal | in name only |
| nominate | name someone for an office |
| nominee | candidate |

THE ROOT **PLAC** MEANS "PLEASURE." WORDS FORMED FROM THIS ROOT INCLUDE **PLACID** (CALM), **COMPLACENT** (SELF-SATISFIED), **IMPLACABLE** (UNAPPEASABLE), **COMPLAISANT** (AMIABLE), AND **PLACATE** (APPEASE).

## EAT UP!

The root *vor* means "eat." If you are a *voracious* eater, you eat everything that isn't nailed down. Here are some other common words that contain the root *vor*.

| Word | Definition |
|---|---|
| carnivore | meat eater |
| frugivore | fruit eater |
| herbivore | plant eater |
| insectivore | insect eater |
| granivore | grain eater |

## BUSY AS A BEAVER

Below are ten Latin roots that pertain to making and doing things.

| Root | Meaning | Example | Definition |
|---|---|---|---|
| dict | say | dictate | authoritative command |
| duct | lead | ductile | easily molded |
| fact | make | factory | place where things are made |

| Root | Meaning | Example | Definition |
|---|---|---|---|
| fer | carry | transfer | carry to another place |
| fic | make/do | petrifaction | being made into stone |
| funct | perform | function | characteristic action |
| grad | go/step | degrade | go down; corrupt |
| ject | throw | reject | throw aside; discard |
| pel, puls | move | impel | urge |
| scrib | write | scribble | scrawl |

## ROOT FOR THE HOME TEAM

In the space provided, write **T** if the definition is true and **F** if it is false. Use what you learned about Latin roots to help you figure out what each word means.

_____ 1. unification union
_____ 2. degradation encouragement
_____ 3. induce influence
_____ 4. jettison bring on board
_____ 5. addiction habit; fixation
_____ 6. gentrification growing old
_____ 7. scribe writer
_____ 8. malediction bad luck
_____ 9. dejected depressed
_____ 10. propellant meddler
_____ 11. contradict dissent; deny
_____ 12. gradient flat surface
_____ 13. inscribe write on
_____ 14. traduce praise
_____ 15. abduct kidnap

It has been estimated that 90 percent of all English words can be traced back to classical Greek, Latin, and Germanic sources.

### ANSWERS

All odd items are true; all even items are false.

## "ONCE MORE UNTO THE BREACH"

This time, match the word to its definition. You may wish to underline the Latin root in each word as you do so. Write your answers in the space provided.

______ 1. abdication a. overpass
______ 2. diversification b. guess

| | |
|---|---|
| ______ 3. repulsion | c. variety |
| ______ 4. benediction | d. decree; order |
| ______ 5. edict | e. renounce a throne |
| ______ 6. misconduct | f. assembly; caucus |
| ______ 7. viaduct | g. undesirable |
| ______ 8. congress | h. aversion |
| ______ 9. conjecture | i. wrongdoing |
| ______ 10. objectionable | j. blessing |

### ANSWERS

| | |
|---|---|
| 1. e | 6. i |
| 2. c | 7. a |
| 3. h | 8. f |
| 4. j | 9. b |
| 5. d | 10. g |

## GETTING BACK TO YOUR ROOTS

Here are fifteen more Latin roots that describe size and amount. Study the roots, examples, and definitions. In some examples, the root is in the prefix position. How would you use some of these words in your daily life?

| Root | Meaning | Example | Definition |
|---|---|---|---|
| alt | high | altitude | height above surface |
| ann | year | annual | yearly |
| brev | short | abbreviation | shortened form |
| centr | center | centrist | moderate viewpoint |
| dors | back | dorsal | back fin |
| fin, term | final | terminus | end |
| magni | large | magnify | grow larger |
| med | middle | medial | in the middle |
| mult | many | multiply | increase |
| nihil | nothing | annihilate | kill |
| omni | all | omnipotent | all-powerful |
| pend | weigh | pendant | hanging ornament |
| sed, sess | sit | sedate | quiet |

| Root | Meaning | Example | Definition |
|---|---|---|---|
| ten, tin | hold | tenet | belief held as true |
| vid, vis | see | provide | get ready before |

## Push the Envelope

Define each word, using its root and what you learned in Chapter 2 about prefixes to help you. Write your definition on the line provided.

1. compendium
2. biennial
3. continence
4. append
5. omniscient
6. supersede
7. pendulous
8. invidious
9. secede
10. omnivorous

### Answers

1. a digest; synopsis; collection
2. happening every two years
3. self-control
4. add to
5. know all things
6. go beyond; replace
7. hanging
8. causing resentment
9. withdraw; resign
10. eating all kinds of foods

The English writer John Dryden (1631–1700) named 1666 "Annus Mirabilis," the Year of Wonders, to commemorate the English victory over the Dutch and the Great Fire of London. What root do you see in **Annus**?

# CHAPTER 4

# BRING UP THE REAR: LEARN SUFFIXES

YOU MUST REMEMBER THIS

A suffix is a letter or group of letters added to the end of a word or root to change the word's meaning.

ALL THE RIGHT MOVES

Suffixes determine a word's part of speech—whether it is used as a noun, verb, adjective, or adverb.

Back in 1780, John Adams urged the creation of an American academy with a lofty charge: to keep the English language "pure." The Continental Congress, preoccupied with more pressing issues (such as securing independence from the Mother Country) let the idea die. They were a wise bunch, that Continental Congress. Trying to keep English "pure" would have been like locking the barn door once the cow was out.

And why would we want English to be "pure"? Poet Carl Sandburg said, "The English language hasn't got where it is by being pure." And a good thing for us, too. Otherwise, how could we justify borrowing all those prefixes, roots, and suffixes from Greek, Latin, and other sources?

In this chapter, you'll learn all about *suffixes,* which are one or more letters that are added to the end of a word to change its meaning.

## TEST YOURSELF

How good are you at using suffixes to decipher words? Find out by completing the following self-test. Each word ends with a suffix. Use what you already know about suffixes to see how many of these words you can decode. Select the correct meaning for each **boldfaced** word. Write the letter of your choice in the space provided.

_____1. **culinary**
a. cute; attractive
b. picky
c. dealing with cooking
d. dealing with cue balls

_____2. **insignificant**
a. momentous
b. sign; insignia
c. consequential
d. unimportant

_____3. **palatial**
a. luxurious
b. incomplete
c. roof of the mouth
d. toothy

_____4. **seditious**
a. rebellious
b. cooperative
c. mutual
d. planted

_____5. **intransigent**
a. not traveling
b. insolvent
c. handsome
d. uncompromising

_____6. **erudite**
a. ruddy-skinned
b. pencil lead
c. knowledgeable
d. dull

_____7. **apothecary**
a. pharmacist
b. fake doctor
c. heavy burden
d. highest point

_____8. **partisan**
a. windmill
b. section
c. supporter
d. navigator

PREFIXES AND SUFFIXES ARE CALLED AFFIXES BECAUSE THEY ARE ADDED TO A ROOT TO PRODUCE A NEW WORD.

_____9. **preponderance**

a. minority
b. majority
c. immaturity
d. overweight

_____10. **mercenary**

a. generous
b. greedy
c. ugly
d. drafty

**ANSWERS**

| | |
|---|---|
| 1. c | 6. c |
| 2. d | 7. a |
| 3. a | 8. c |
| 4. a | 9. b |
| 5. d | 10. b |

## ALL'S WELL THAT ENDS WELL

As you learned in the beginning of this chapter, suffixes can affect how a word functions in a sentence. For instance:

- Suffixes can change a word's part of speech.

**Example:** Adding a suffix can change a verb to an adjective, as in *risk* to *risky*.

- Suffixes can change a word's tense (or time).

**Example:** Add -d or -ed to make a present-tense verb into a past-tense verb.

| **Present tense** | **Past tense** |
|---|---|
| live | lived |
| fasten | fastened |

- Suffixes can change a word's meaning.

**Example:** *Kitchen* becomes *kitchenette*. The diminutive *-ette*, meaning "little one," shows a smaller version of a person, place, or thing (*cigar to cigarette*).

Just as knowing a small number of prefixes and roots can help you figure out many unfamiliar words, so knowing a few everyday suffixes can help you add many useful words to your vocabulary.

## TO BE OR NOT TO BE

Below are twelve suffixes that describe a state of being. How many more words can you think of that end with these suffixes?

| Suffix | Example |
|---|---|
| 1. -ance | appearance |
| 2. -ant | deviant |
| 3. -cy | infancy |
| 4. -dom | freedom |
| 5. -ence | independence |
| 6. -ent | corpulent |
| 7. -hood | neighborhood |
| 8. -mony | matrimony |
| 9. -ness | lightness |
| 10. -sis | thesis |
| 11. -tic | gigantic |
| 12. -ty | novelty |

LEARNING PREFIXES, ROOTS, AND SUFFIXES CAN HELP YOU UNDERSTAND PROFESSIONAL, TECHNICAL, AND ACADEMIC VOCABULARY, WHERE GREEK AND LATIN SOURCES ARE VERY COMMON.

## END ZONE

Assess what you've learned about suffixes that describe a state of being by completing the following chart. For each word, first write the suffix and its meaning. Then use what you've learned about suffixes to define each word. Don't hesitate to look back at what you just learned or to use a dictionary if you would like to.

| Word | Suffix | Meaning | Word Meaning |
|---|---|---|---|
| 1. goodness | | | |
| 2. anxiety | | | |
| 3. brilliance | | | |
| 4. despondence | | | |
| 5. catharsis | | | |
| 6. effulgent | | | |
| 7. hypothesis | | | |
| 8. resilient | | | |
| 9. repellent | | | |
| 10. officialdom | | | |
| 11. thrifty | | | |
| 12. complacency | | | |
| 13. truculent | | | |

14. brotherhood

15. convalescence

16. adamant

17. diligent

18. parity

19. disenchant

20. ambivalent

## ANSWERS

| Word | Suffix | Meaning | Word Meaning |
|---|---|---|---|
| 1. goodness | -ness | state of being | being good |
| 2. anxiety | -ty | state of being | nervousness |
| 3. brilliance | -ance | state of being | brightness |
| 4. despondence | -ence | state of being | sadness |
| 5. catharsis | -sis | state of being | purging |
| 6. effulgent | -ent | state of being | flowing |
| 7. hypothesis | -sis | state of being | assumption |
| 8. resilient | -ent | state of being | elastic |
| 9. repellent | -ent | state of being | offensive |
| 10. kingdom | -dom | state of being | monarchy |
| 11. thrifty | -ty | state of being | economical |
| 12. complacency | -cy | state of being | quiet satisfaction |
| 13. truculent | -ent | state of being | harsh |
| 14. brotherhood | -hood | state of being | friendship |
| 15. convalescence | -ence | state of being | recovering |
| 16. adamant | -ant | state of being | definite |
| 17. diligent | -ent | state of being | hard working |
| 18. parity | -ty | state of being | equality |
| 19. disenchant | -ant | state of being | disillusion |
| 20. ambivalent | -ent | state of being | unsure |

## WHEELER DEALER

A *lawyer* is someone who deals with the law; a *buyer* is someone who buys items. Below are nine more suffixes that indicate a person who is something, does something, or deals with something.

| Suffix | Example |
|---|---|
| -ar | scholar |
| -ard | dullard |
| -ary | revolutionary |
| -er | worker |
| -ian | historian |
| -ier | furrier |
| -ist | psychologist |
| -ite | socialite |
| -or | bettor |

## SWEET ENDINGS

This time, match the word to its definition. If you wish, underline the suffix in each word to help you remember how it is used. Write your answers in the space provided.

| | |
|---|---|
| ________1. functionary | a. philosopher, scholar |
| ________2. editor | b. settled |
| ________3. taxidermist | c. person who edits |
| ________4. comedian | d. mediator |
| ________5. arbitrator | e. an official |
| ________6. pedestrian | f. opponent |
| ________7. theorist | g. handwriting |
| ________8. adversary | h. person who stuffs dead animals |
| ________9. sedentary | i. person who walks |
| ________10. penmanship | j. humorist |

## Answers

| | |
|---|---|
| 1. e | 6. i |
| 2. c | 7. a |
| 3. h | 8. f |
| 4. j | 9. b |
| 5. d | 10. g |

> MANY USEFUL WORDS HAVE BEEN FORMED WITH THE SUFFIX **-IST**. OFTEN, THESE WORDS DESCRIBE HOBBIES OR CAREERS. FOR EXAMPLE, A **NUMISMATIST** DEALS WITH COINS; A **PHILATELIST** DEALS WITH STAMPS. AN **ARBORIST** DEALS WITH TREE CARE; AN **ENTOMOLOGIST**, WITH INSECTS. A **GENETICIST** DEALS WITH HEREDITY; A **METEOROLOGIST**, WITH THE WEATHER.

## Walk This Way

Below are twelve suffixes that all mean "resembling, like, or of." Study them and the examples. Then complete the activity that follows to help you incorporate these words and suffixes into your daily vocabulary.

| **Suffix** | **Example** |
|---|---|
| -ac | cardiac |
| -al | natural |
| -an | suburban |
| -esque | Lincolnesque |
| -ile | infantile |
| -ine | masculine |
| -ish | foolish |
| -ly | yearly |
| -ory | advisory |
| -oid | android (humanlike) |
| -some | worrisome |
| -wise | likewise |

> THE SUFFIXES **-ARIUM** AND **-ARY** REFER TO "PLACE," AS THESE EXAMPLES SHOW: **AQUARIUM, SOLARIUM, LIBRARY,** AND **AVIARY**.

## Truth or Dare

In the space provided, write **T** if the definition is true and **F** if it is false. Use what you learned about suffixes that mean "*resembling, like*, or *of*" to help you figure out what each word means.

_____ 1. devilish — like a devil
_____ 2. cuboid — like a cube

| | | |
|---|---|---|
| _____ | 3. puerile | childish |
| _____ | 4. saturnine | sluggish, gloomy |
| _____ | 5. fulsome | shortage |
| _____ | 6. sensory | pertaining to the senses |
| _____ | 7. Romanesque | like the Romans |
| _____ | 8. pastoral | wild, untamed |
| _____ | 9. ovoid | like an egg |
| _____ | 10. dollarwise | pertaining to money |
| _____ | 11. fictional | factual |
| _____ | 12. churlish | polite |

### ANSWERS

| | | |
|---|---|---|
| 1. T | 5. F | 9. T |
| 2. T | 6. T | 10. T |
| 3. T | 7. T | 11. F |
| 4. T | 8. F | 12. F |

## HOW MUCH IS THAT DOGGY IN THE WINDOW?

We don't want to forget suffixes that show **amount**, such as -y, which means "full of." Thanks to that little -y, we get such words as *risky*, *weary*, and *wily*.

Below are ten more suffixes that show amount. Study them and the examples to help your vocabulary grow by leaps and bounds.

| **Suffix** | **Meaning** | **Example** |
|---|---|---|
| -aceous | having | curvaceous |
| -ed | characterized by | cultured |
| -lent | inclined to be | prevalent |
| -ose | full of | verbose |
| -ous | full of | perilous |
| -ious | having | vicious |
| -less | without | guiltless |
| -ling | minor | yearling |
| -fold | increased by | tenfold |
| -ful | full | healthful |

WHAT DO THE FOLLOWING FOUR WORDS HAVE IN COMMON: **REGULATE, PASSIONATE, COLLEGIATE,** AND **AFFECTIONATE?** (ANSWER: THEY ALL END WITH THE SUFFIX **-ATE.**)

## END RUN

Define each word, using its suffix to help you decode it. Write your definition on the line provided.

1. careless
2. abstemious
3. masterful
4. mendacious
5. noxious
6. malevolent
7. manifold
8. bigoted
9. helpless
10. carbonaceous

### ANSWERS

1. reckless
2. self-restrained, sober
3. commanding
4. lying
5. harmful
6. evil
7. many
8. prejudiced
9. defenseless
10. full of carbon

## DO IT YOURSELF

The following four suffixes are for do-it-yourself types. That's because each one means "to make or do." They can all help you build better words!

| Suffix | Example | Definition |
|---|---|---|
| -ate | alienate | to make alien |
| | liberate | to make free |
| -en | weaken | to make weak |
| | moisten | to make moist |

| | | |
|---|---|---|
| -ite | unite | to make one |
| | ignite | to make light |
| -ize | visualize | to make visible |
| | sanitize | to make clean |

ARE YOU FEELING **CAPABLE** TODAY? THEN THE SUFFIXES **-ABLE** AND **-IBLE** ARE FOR YOU! THEY LET YOU FORM SUCH "CAPABLE" WORDS AS **AFFORDABLE, LOVABLE, COMBUSTIBLE,** AND **INCREDIBLE.**

## ACT UP!

Here are six suffixes that all have to do with action. Which ones have you seen before?

| Suffix | Example |
|---|---|
| -age | marriage |
| -ation | allegation |
| -ing | meeting |
| -ion | rebellion |
| -ition | recognition |
| -tion | commotion |

## MATCHMAKER, MATCHMAKER

Make a match by drawing a line to connect the vocabulary word to its definition. If you wish, underline the suffix in each word to help you remember how it is used.

| | |
|---|---|
| 1. ablution | a. act of talking |
| 2. affirmation | b. act of collecting and assembling in order |
| 3. carnage | c. act of racking up miles |
| 4. collating | d. act of supporting |
| 5. conversation | e. act of killing |
| 6. convocation | f. act of producing |
| 7. mileage | g. act of being a pilgrim |
| 8. operation | h. act of coming together |
| 9. patronage | i. act of agreeing |
| 10. pilgrimage | j. act of washing |

THE SUFFIX **-IC**, MEANING "ASSOCIATED WITH," IS ESPECIALLY USEFUL. IT HAS LET US MAKE SUCH EVERYDAY WORDS AS **DEMOCRATIC, ANGELIC, INORGANIC, TITANIC, PSYCHOPATHIC, CRYPTIC,** AND **BUCOLIC.**

## ANSWERS

1. j 2. i 3. e 4. b 5. a
6. h 7. c 8. f 9. d 10. g

## GRAB BAG

Let's finish up with fifteen suffixes that crop up in many of the words and expressions you use every day.

| Suffix | Meaning | Example |
|---|---|---|
| -erly | to, directly | easterly |
| -escent | beginning | opalescent |
| -eum | place for | museum |
| -ferous | carrying, bearing | odoriferous |
| -ia | condition | anorexia |
| -fy | marked by | magnify |
| -ical | having to do with | musical |
| -id | inclined to be | florid |
| -ive | inclined to be | festive |
| -ism | practice, quality | baptism |
| -itis | inflammation | arthritis |
| -ment | result of | judgment |
| -tude | condition | rectitude |
| -ure | means, quality | rapture |
| -ward | to | sideward |

## END GAME

Match each word in the first column to its definition in the second column. If you wish, underline the suffix in each word to help you remember how it is used. Write your answers in the space provided.

_____ 1. appendicitis a. eager
_____ 2. discernment b. intend
_____ 3. nihilism c. surrender

| | | |
|---|---|---|
| _____ | 4. adolescent | d. inflammation of appendix |
| _____ | 5. expenditures | e. open-air theater |
| _____ | 6. abandonment | f. insight |
| _____ | 7. heroism | g. reversion; throwback |
| _____ | 8. inducement | h. strengthen |
| _____ | 9. intensify | i. expenses |
| _____ | 10. signify | j. bravery |
| _____ | 11. coliseum | k. teen |
| _____ | 12. obsolescent | l. unusable |
| _____ | 13. fervid | m. belief that life is senseless |
| _____ | 14. sinusitis | n. inflammation of sinuses |
| _____ | 15. atavism | o. motive |

### ANSWERS

| | | |
|---|---|---|
| 1. d | 6. c | 11. e |
| 2. f | 7. j | 12. l |
| 3. m | 8. o | 13. a |
| 4. k | 9. h | 14. n |
| 5. i | 10. b | 15. g |

## END OF THE LINE

How about one final self-test to tie it together? Select the correct meaning for each of the following **boldfaced** words. Circle your choice.

1. **certainty**

   incredulous  sureness  rigidity

2. **clownish**

   admirable  humorous  foolish

3. **intermediary**

   middle man  middle-aged  midpoint

4. **chromosomal**

   genetic  abnormal  contagious

5. **transparent**
   clean | clear | commendable

6. **assiduity**
   preposterousness | persistence | determination

7. **castigate**
   to put in a cast | to rebuke | to praise

8. **modesty**
   audacity | humility | fashionable

9. **terrarium**
   an environment for land animals | an environment for extinct creatures | a shallow pool

10. **abstinent**
   stubborn | sober | intoxicated

11. **glamorous**
   famous | alluring | obscure

12. **visionary**
   idealist | practicable | wealthy

13. **terminate**
   begin | end | murder

14. **waspish**
   testy | cheerful | ugly

15. **accidental**
   on purpose | by chance | planned

16. **engraved**
   image | carved in | worship

17. **victorious**
   triumphant | surrender | screeching

18. **proselytize**

| try to convert | try to eat | try to sleep |
|---|---|---|

19. **conical**

| square-shaped | cone-shaped | copier |
|---|---|---|

20. **gracious**

| curt | coarse | courteous |
|---|---|---|

21. **lachrymose**

| weepy | jubilant | lazy |
|---|---|---|

22. **culpable**

| able to swallow | liable | able to cope |
|---|---|---|

23. **recapitulate**

| decapitate | twist | summarize |
|---|---|---|

24. **tonsillitis**

| inflammation of the tonsils | inflammation of the scalp | silly behavior |
|---|---|---|

25. **indescribable**

| inedible | warped | astonishing |
|---|---|---|

## ANSWERS

1. sureness
2. foolish
3. middle man
4. genetic
5. clear
6. persistence
7. rebuke
8. humility
9. an environment for land animals
10. sober
11. alluring
12. idealist
13. end
14. testy
15. by chance
16. carved in
17. triumphant
18. try to convert
19. cone-shaped
20. courteous
21. weepy
22. liable
23. summarize
24. inflammation of the tonsils
25. astonishing

# CHAPTER 5

# IT'S ALL IN THE PACKAGING: CONTEXT CLUES

YOU MUST REMEMBER THIS

You can often define an unfamiliar word by the information surrounding it—the word's *context*.

ALL THE RIGHT MOVES

The unfamiliar word may be defined right in the text, or you will have to infer the meaning from what you already know and from details you have heard or read.

Let's say you come across this passage in your reading:

> Long-time Boston residents still talk about the molasses flood that *engulfed* the city's North End on January 15, 1919. Hundreds of people were sitting near the Purity Distilling Corporation's 50 foot high molasses tank—and it was about to split apart. The metal bolts popped out, the seams burst, and tons of molasses erupted out in a surge of deadly goo.

"Engulfed," you say. "Never heard that word before."

Now, you *could* get the dictionary, but that would mean getting up and walking all the way across the room. You're settled in the chair just right, so why get up? Instead, why not try to figure out the meaning of *engulf* from the words around it?

If a 50 foot molasses tank burst and sent "tons of molasses erupt(ing) out in a surge of deadly goo," *engulfed* must mean "to drown or flood." And so it does.

Many times, you can get clues to the meaning of unfamiliar words by the information surrounding the words—the *context.* This means that you can often interpret a word's specific meaning by examining its relationship to other words in the sentence. To add power to your speech and writing, you must understand how a word interacts with other words. Although context can sometimes be as unreliable as the bus, many times it can come through in spectacular ways. That's what you'll learn in this chapter.

## HIDDEN IN PLAIN SIGHT

Writers want their words to be understood so their message gets across. As a result, they will often define a difficult word right in the text. For example, here's how one writer defined the word *levee:*

> The Army Corps of Engineers distributed 26 million plastic bags throughout the region. Volunteers filled each bag with 35 pounds of sand and then stacked them to create *levees*, makeshift barriers against the floodwaters.

Right after the word *levee*, readers get the definition: "makeshift barriers against the floodwaters."

Here's another example. In this instance, the writer defines *tsunami:*

> During a tidal wave, a wall of water 25 feet high can rush to shore, pushed by 200-mile-per-hour winds. Called *tsunamis*, these fierce tidal waves strike the shore with tremendous force and cause considerable damage to life and property.

Again, the definition follows right after the word. As a result, readers learn that *tsunamis* are "fierce tidal waves."

## HIDE AND SEEK

In each of the following examples, the writer has provided the definition for a challenging vocabulary word. Read each passage. Then circle the definition of each **boldfaced** word.

1. In many Native American tribes, the **shaman**, or medicine man, acted as a ceremonial priest.

2. As with all electric **currents**, or discharges, lightning will follow the path of least resistance. This means that it will take the route that is easiest to travel on.

3. Many settlers on the vast American plains in the late nineteenth century used **sod**, or earth, as a building material for their houses.

4. Then, arrange a handful of **mulch**, dead leaves, on the top of the soil.

5. Born in 1833, John Styth Pemberton was a **pharmacist**, a drug store owner, who moved to Atlanta, Georgia, in 1869.

6. To make a living, he created so-called **patent medicines**, homemade medicines that were sold without a prescription.

7. Since many large companies have **downsized**, reduced their staffs, there are fewer management and support jobs available.

8. We crunch and chew our way through vast quantities of snacks and **confectioneries**, candies, and relieve our thirst with multicolored, flavored soft drinks.

9. Ophthalmologists and optometrists are both eye-care specialists, but there are differences between what they can do. **Ophthalmologists** are specialists who are also medical doctors. They have earned their M.D. degrees.

10. **Optometrists** are not medical doctors. However, they can test vision and prescribe and sell eyeglasses and contact lenses because they have earned optometry degrees in eye care.

### ANSWERS

1. medicine man
2. discharges: the route that is easiest
3. earth
4. dead leaves
5. a drugstore owner
6. homemade medicines that were sold without a prescription
7. the reduction of a company's staff
8. candies
9. eye-care specialists who are medical doctors
10. eye-care specialists who are not medical doctors

## DOT'S IT

Writers often use a colon (:) to introduce a passage that explains a word mentioned earlier in the sentence. Often, too, a colon introduces a list of things that helps define or elaborate on a word. Read the colon as the phrase "as follows."

Here are three examples:

> Some people claim that the 1990s is the decade of fitness. But in fact, at least one-third of the American population is classified as *obese:* being more than 20 percent over a person's ideal body weight.

Right after the colon, the writer defines obese, "being more than 20 percent over a person's ideal body weight." Here's another example of this context clue technique:

> On the slide, we saw that a drop of water contained *bacteria:* one-celled organisms that are too small to be seen by the naked eye.

Again, right after the colon the writer defines bacteria. They are "one-celled organisms that are too small to be seen by the naked eye."

> Santa Anna had brought with him several objects from home, including a large lump of *chicle:* the elastic sap of the sapodilla tree.

What's *chicle*? The writer tells us that it's the elastic sap of the sapodilla tree.

## ONE IF BY LAND, TWO IF BY SEA

Writers and speakers may signal you that more information about an unfamiliar word is coming down the pike. Here are three of the most common signals for additional information:

**for example** = **that is** + **in other words**

Look for these phrases because the definition of a tricky word often follows them. Let's see how it works with the following example:

> One symptom of the condition is *lethargy;* for example, a feeling of passivity and inactivity.

The definition of *lethargy*—"a feeling of passivity and inactivity"—is right after the phrase "for example." Here's another example:

> In 1869, Antonio Lopez de Santa Anna, the brave Mexican leader of the Alamo attack, had been sent into *exile*; that is, he was banished from his country. He ended up on Staten Island, New York.

The definition of *exile*—"banishment"—comes right after the phrase "that is." One final example:

> Sharks are models of efficiency with their boneless skeletons, simple brains, generalized nervous systems, and simple internal structures. Their hydrodynamically designed shapes, razor-sharp replaceable teeth, powerful jaws, and greedy appetites make them excellent *marauders*; in other words, brutal raiders.

The definition of *marauders*—"brutal raiders"—comes right after the phrase "in other words."

## ARMCHAIR DETECTIVE

In the best of all possible worlds, the writer or speaker would always, immediately define any unfamiliar word. As you well know, this is not the best of all possible worlds. One of the signs? Just check out all the undefined words floating around. You can nab these toughies. Use your detective skills to figure out what any unfamiliar word means.

In these instances, you'll be making *inferences*. This means that you'll make a logical connection or fill in information that is not spelled out. People call this "putting two and two together" or "reading between the lines." Your clues are the information that you already know and the details that you are given in the sentence or paragraph.

Study this equation:

**What you already know + context details = definition**

Let's give it a whirl with these examples:

> Here's how you could get rich: Start a women's clothing store called "Size 2," in which all garments, including those that were originally intended to be

restaurant awnings, had labels with the words "Size 2." I bet you'd sell clothes like crazy. You'd probably get rich, and you could retire, maybe take up some *philanthropic* activity to benefit humanity.

| **What you already know +** | **context details =** | **definition** |
|---|---|---|
| Philo means "love" | philanthropic activities | "benefit humanity" |

You can infer from what you already know and from context clues that a *philanthropic* activity must be something that is good for humankind, such as a charity.

THE SIGNAL WORDS **AS** AND **BECAUSE** SHOW CAUSE OR REASON.

Here's another example:

> In 1862, in order to support the Civil War effort, Congress enacted the nation's first income tax law. It was a *forerunner* of our modern income tax in that it was based on the principles of graduated, or progressive taxation, and of withholding income at the source.

| **What you already know +** | **context details =** | **definition** |
|---|---|---|
| *Fore* means "before" | The forerunner was | the "nation's first income tax law." |

Therefore, you can infer from what you already know and context clues that *forerunner* means "come before or precede."

One final example:

> Each year about twenty-five to thirty shark attacks on people are reported worldwide with the victims either maimed or killed. Research on shark attacks may eventually lead to the development of an effective shark *repellent*.

| **What you already know +** | **context details =** | **definition** |
|---|---|---|
| *Repel* means "turn back" | shark repellent | Researchers are looking for a way to stop sharks from attacking people. |

Combining what you already know with context clues, you can infer that a *repellent* is something that drives away sharks.

## YOUR TURN

Use what you already know and context clues to figure out the meaning of each of the underlined words in the following passages.

1. After an interminable time of moving one car length a minute at the New Jersey Turnpike exit for the Goethals Bridge, I saw the following handwritten explanation taped to the tollbooth door: "The traffic is due to a high volume of cars." The answers are so simple sometimes, aren't they?

*Interminable* means ______________________________
Context clue:______________________________

2. Why is yawning contagious? You yawn to equalize the pressure on your eardrums. One might think the pressure change outside your eardrums destabilizes other people's ear pressure, so they must yawn to even it out.

*Contagious* means ______________________________
Context clue: ______________________________

3. The earth may spin faster on its axis due to deforestation. Just as a figure skater's rate of spin increases when the arms are brought in close to the body, the cutting of tall trees may cause our planet to spin dangerously fast.

*Deforestation* means ______________________________
Context clue: ______________________________

4. A man in York, England, signed up for the Special Olympics competition and won several events, including a wheelchair discus throw. The man was disqualified, however, when several people recognized him as their mailman, a perfectly healthy fellow. When asked about the ruse, the man explained, "It's all a mistake. I'm sick."

*Ruse* means ______________________________
Context clue: ______________________________

5. Potatoes are nourishing. The Irish population, which lived almost solely on potatoes, nearly tripled from the middle of the eighteenth century to just about the middle of the nineteenth century.

*Nourishing* means ______________________________
Context clue: ______________________________

6. Tornadoes can be perilous. Since tornadoes can pick up a house and drop it hundreds of feet away, these are extremely dangerous storms.

*Perilous* means ______________________________
Context clue: ______________________________

7. Earthquakes continue to kill in some areas at a level usually reserved for wars and epidemics. Eleven thousand people died in northeastern Iran on August 31, 1968—not that long ago. Nor is the heavy death toll of a lethal earthquake the end of the disaster.

*Lethal* means ______________________________
Context clue: ______________________________

8. While many sharks are caught by fishermen for sport, sharks can and do sustain small commercial ventures. For example, their skins provide a hide tougher than leather, out of which boots and wallets are fabricated.

*Fabricated* means ______________________________
Context clue: ______________________________

9. Shark meat is processed for human consumption. The British "fish-and-chips" industry depends on shark meat; the Italians annually consume about 10 million pounds of smooth dogfish shark; the Chinese use shark fins for soup.

*Consumption* means ______________________________
Context clue: ______________________________

10. Paleontologists, scientists who study extinct forms of animal life, once thought that dinosaurs had such small, inefficient brains that they were somehow responsible for their own dying out.

*Extinct* means ______________________________
Context clue: ______________________________

## ANSWERS

1. definition: without end
   context clue: "moving one car length a minute"
2. definition: catching
   context clue: "other people's ear pressure, so they must yawn"
3. definition: removing forests
   context clue: "cutting of tall trees"
4. definition: trick, stratagem
   context clue: "The man was disqualified, however, when several people recognized him as their mailman, a perfectly healthy fellow."
5. definition: "good for you"
   context clue: If the population "nearly tripled," nourishing must mean "helps people to grow"—and it does.
6. definition: extremely dangerous
   context clue: "extremely dangerous"
7. definition: deadly
   context clue: "heavy death toll"
8. definition: made, produced, created
   context clues: since boots and wallets are made from their skins, fabricated must mean "produced."
9. definition: eating or using
   context clue: "fish-and-chips," "the Italians annually consume . . . ," and "the Chinese use shark fins for soup."
10. definition: died out
    context clue: "their own dying out"

DON'T BE FOOLED! A SEMICOLON (;) IS NOT THE SAME AS A COLON (:). A SEMICOLON IS USED TO SEPARATE TWO INDEPENDENT CLAUSES (COMPLETE SENTENCES), WHILE THE COLON MAY BE USED TO INTRODUCE A LIST, DEFINITION, OR THE SALUTATION OF A BUSINESS LETTER.

## ONCE MORE WITH GUSTO

Since using context is such an important way to define unfamiliar words, why not practice a little more. Below are ten more **boldfaced** words. Based on its context, select the best definition for each word. Write your answer in the space provided.

_____1. Police in Wichita, Kansas, arrested a twenty-two-year-old man at an airport hotel after he tried to pass two **counterfeit** $16 bills.

a. large　　c. dirty
b. fake, forged　　d. foreign

_____2. By the 1800s, several hundred medicine shows were traveling across America, giving a wide variety of performances. At one end of the scale were simple magic acts; at the other, complicated **spectacles**.

a. large-scale, impressive shows　　c. small shows
b. eyeglasses　　d. tricks

_____3. One of the most **outlandish** figures was the glib "Nevada Ned, the King of Gold." Born Ned T. Oliver, this entertainer wore a fancy suit studded with buttons made of gold.

a. bizarre　　c. well-dressed
b. conservative　　d. rich

_____4. On his head he sported a huge **sombrero** dangling a hundred gold coins.

a. hairpiece　　c. hat
b. toupee　　d. plate

_____5. Fake "medicines," which sold for fifty cents to a dollar per bottle, were guaranteed to cure all the ills that **afflict** the human body.

a. cure　　c. comfort
b. distress　　d. refresh

_____6. There have been many controversial World Series, but the most **infamous** was certainly the thrown World Series of 1919. It took almost a year for three men—Lefty Williams, Eddie Cicotte, and J. Jackson—to sign confessions admitting the series had been fixed and they were in on it.

a. impressive　　c. celebrated
b. important　　d. notorious

_____7. Sensing a sure thing, Jack Doyle, the head of a New York City betting ring, **rigged** the series. Actually, the series seemed quite respectable, with the Reds winning it five games to three.

a. "fixed" in advance
c. set up a mast
b. equipped
d. repaired

_____8. A company trying to continue its five-year perfect safety record showed its workers a film that encouraged the use of safety goggles on the job. According to Industrial Machinery News, the film's depiction of **gory** industrial accidents was so bloody that twenty-five workers suffered minor injuries in their rush to leave the screening room.

a. unnecessary
c. strange
b. gruesome, bloody
d. random

_____9. In the past, a good stereo system consisted of a receiver, speakers, and a turntable, all carefully picked to match the buyer's needs. For the buyer who could not afford to purchase all the separate **components** at once or who did not want the bother of selecting them, manufacturers sold all-in-one stereo systems that had everything a person needed in one package.

a. total package
c. elements, parts
b. sounds
d. filling

_____10. Most natural hazards can be detected before their threat matures. But earthquakes have no known **precursors**, so they come without warning, like the vengeance of an ancient warrior.

a. dangers
c. signs, signals
b. risks
d. gambles

### Answers

| | |
|---|---|
| 1. b | 6. d |
| 2. a | 7. a |
| 3. a | 8. b |
| 4. c | 9. c |
| 5. b | 10. c |

# PART II:

# WORDS TO WATCH

• • • •

**TECH SUPPORT:** ***What does the screen say now?***

**PERSON:** ***It says, "Hit enter when ready."***

**TECH SUPPORT:** ***Well?***

**PERSON:** ***How do I know when it's ready?***

*You're* ready—and you don't even have to hit ENTER. In the second half of this book, you'll learn more easy and valuable ways to increase your everyday vocabulary. These methods include:

- understanding homonyms and homophones
- learning commonly confused words
- exploring word histories
- discovering words from other languages
- mastering words from the professions

# CHAPTER 6

# GIVE PIECE A CHANCE: HOMONYMS AND HOMOPHONES

YOU MUST REMEMBER THIS

*Homonyms* are words with the same spelling and pronunciations but different meanings, such as *bore* and *bore*, *lay* and *lay*, *lie* and *lie*.

*Homophones* are words with the same pronunciation but different spellings and meanings, such as *arc* and *ark*, *weather* and *whether*, *hear* and *here*.

ALL THE RIGHT MOVES

If in doubt, check a dictionary to make sure you've picked the word you want—not its first cousin.

They walk alike, they talk alike; you could lose your mind. Like those classic TV twins Patty and Cathy, some pairs or groups of words are often mistaken for the other. Sometimes it is because the words sound alike; other times it is because they are spelled alike but carry different meanings. In either event, distinguishing between these confusing words is crucial because it helps you write exactly what you mean. Keeping these partners in crime separate can also save you some needless embarrassment.

The prime offenders are called *homonyms* and *homophones*. *Homonyms* are words with the same spelling and pronunciations but different meanings, such as *bay* and *bay* or *beam* and *beam*. *Homophones* are words with the same pronunciation but different spellings and meanings, such as *coarse* and *course* or *bridal* and *bridle*. In general, homophones are more common than homonyms.

Homonyms and homophones are like the bad boys in the back row of homeroom, the ones you want to send to detention. Like unruly boys, there's no easy way to deal with these naughty words. The best you can do is memorize them. That way, you can instantly recognize the ones that drive you around the bend. This chapter will help you recognize all these tricky vocabulary words.

Let's see where you stand before we decide where you have to go. Complete each of the following sentences by circling the correct word in parentheses.

1. America is a large, friendly dog in a small room. Every time it wags its (tale, tail) it knocks over a chair.

2. Some mornings, it's just not worth fighting (threw, through) the crowded streets.

3. A cucumber should be well sliced, dressed with salt and pepper, and then (throne, thrown) out.

4. Police in Wichita, Kansas, arrested a twenty-two-year-old man at an airport hotel after he tried to pass (to, too, two) counterfeit $16 bills.

5. Every time she visited her grandmother for the holidays, her (waste, waist) paid the price.

6. Not a (weak, week) goes by that he doesn't think about her.

7. The feud between the families continues. It all started over the usual: who controls what, who insulted whom, (weather, whether) the holiday meal will be held in a restaurant or at home.

8. Two farmers each claimed to own a certain cow. While one pulled on its head and the other pulled on its (tale, tail), the cow was milked by a machine.

9. Martin Buser won his third Iditarod title in the grueling Alaskan dog-sled race. However, the team from Beverly Hills has yet to finish. Apparently, French poodles weren't the (weigh, way) to go.

10. Archeologist: a person (who's, whose) career lies in ruins.

11. There is never enough time—unless (your, you're) serving it.

## ANSWERS

In each case, the last word in parentheses is correct.

Now it's time to bite the bullet and learn to distinguish these words from their buddies. Here, then, are ten of the worst offenders:

1. **air**: atmosphere
   There's no air in a vacuum—hence his empty head.

   **err**: make a mistake
   To err is human; to purr, feline.

2. **a lot**: many
   The new store gets a lot of business because it offers high-quality merchandise at fair prices.

   **allot**: divide
   Allot the ping-pong balls, mayonnaise, and video equipment equally among all participants, please.

3. **altar**: a platform upon which religious rites are performed
   The priest placed the prayer book on the altar.

   **alter**: change
   Fashion is a form of ugliness so intolerable that we have to alter it every six months.

4. **allowed**: given permission
   Democracy is being allowed to vote for the candidate you dislike least.

   **aloud**: out loud, verbally
   Don't say it aloud. Don't even think it quietly.

5. **hour**: the 24th part of the day
   "Shape your heart to front the hour, but dream not that the hour will last."
   —Alfred, Lord Tennyson

**our**: belonging to us

Television is more interesting than people. If it were not, we would have a lot of people standing in the corners of our living rooms.

6. **bare**: undressed

The doll was bare before the little girl dressed it.

**bare**: unadorned, plain

Just take the bare essentials when you go camping: a hair dryer, an espresso machine, and the TV satellite dish.

**bear:** fuzzy-wuzzy animal

Woody Allen claimed that his parents put a live teddy bear in his crib.

**bear**: carry, hold

I bear no grudges; I have a mind that retains nothing.

7. **born**: native, brought forth by birth

Born free . . . taxed to death.

**borne**: endured (past participle of "to bear")

Lucia had borne his insults as well as she could, but when he slandered her pet duck Quackers, she vowed revenge.

8. **bore**: tiresome person

A bore is someone who, when you ask him how he is, tells you.

**boar**: male pig

The little boys in William Golding's novel *Lord of the Flies* did some odd things with the boar they found in the woods.

9. **brake**: to retard or stop

Warning: I brake for no apparent reason.

**break**: to crack or destroy

Don't break my back.

10. **breadth**: the measure of the side-to-side dimension of an object

Call that a carry-on bag? It has a breadth of more than 6 feet!

**breath**: inhalation and exhalation

The baby drew its first <u>breath</u> with a loud cry.

## Top of Your Game

Take a break (not a *brake*) and complete the following itty-bitty little quiz. Circle the correct choice in each sentence. Some sentences may have more than one homophone.

1. To (air, err) is human, to forgive divine.
2. You need to save (allot, a lot) of money to afford a new car today.
3. Some people should just not be (aloud, allowed) to speak (allowed, aloud).
4. Jack was (born, borne) in a hospital in Newport, Rhode Island.
5. (Our, Hour) cats intended to teach us that not everything in nature has a function.
6. There are two kinds of (err, air) travel in the United States: first class and third world.
7. Think I was (born, borne) yesterday?
8. My date was such a (bore, boar) that he put even himself to sleep.
9. Smokey the (Bare, Bear) warns us not to start forest fires.
10. "It's (are, our) fault we're late," the man said. "We took too long eating dinner."

### Answers

| | | | |
|---|---|---|---|
| 1. err | 4. born | 7. born | 10. our |
| 2. a lot | 5. Our | 8. bore | |
| 3. allowed, aloud | 6. air | 9. Bear | |

Below are ten often confused word pairs. Use a dictionary to help you define each word. (Don't panic; answers follow.)

1. *all together:*

*altogether:*

2. *already:*

*all ready:*

3. *arc:*

*ark:*

4. *ascent:*

*assent:*

5. *base:*

*bass:*

6. *beau:*

*bow:*

7. *berth:*

*birth:*

8. *board:*

*bored:*

9. *bread:*

*bred:*

10. *bridal:*

*bridle:*

## Answers

1. *all together*: all at one time
   *altogether*: completely
2. *already*: previously
   *all ready*: completely prepared
3. *arc*: part of the circumference of a circle; curved line
   *ark*: boat
4. *ascent*: to move up
   *assent*: to agree
5. *base*: the bottom part of an object; the plate in baseball; morally low
   *bass*: the lowest male voice; a type of fish; a musical instrument
6. *beau*: sweetheart
   *bow*: a device used to propel arrows; loops of ribbon; the forward end of a ship
7. *berth*: a sleeping area in a ship
   *birth*: being born
8. *board*: a thin piece of wood; a group of directors
   *bored*: not interested
9. *bread*: baked goods
   *bred*: to cause to be born (past participle of "to breed")
10. *bridal*: pertaining to the bride or a wedding
    *bridle*: part of a horse's harness

## Confusion: An Order Which is Not Understood

My turn. Here are ten more nifty word pairs that are often confused:

1. *buy*: to purchase
   Buy good clothes. They will last longer than cheaply made items.

   *by*: near or next to
   The lime-green exercise shorts are by the exercise machines, way across the room from the pastry.

2. *capital*: the city or town that is the official seat of government; highly important; net worth of a business
   The capital of New York State is Albany.

   *Capitol*: any building in which a legislative body meets
   There's a shiny gold dome on the Capitol building in Washington D.C.

3. *duel*: combat between two people
   The duel was fought at the break of dawn.

   *dual*: reference to two
   The hairband served a dual purpose: fashion and function.

4. *cell*: a small room, as in a convent or prison
   The prisoner's cell was small, cold and dark.

   *sell*: to trade
   The owner decided to sell the rare, valuable coins.

5. *cent*: a penny
   Fifteen cents of every thirty-two-cent stamp goes for storage.

   *scent*: aroma
   What a lovely scent the flower has!

6. *cheep*: what a bird says
   "Cheep, cheep," said the canary.

   *cheap*: not expensive
   Talk is cheap because supply exceeds demand.

7. *deer*: animal
   The deer sneered at the inept hunter.

   *dear*: beloved
   Groucho Marx said to one of his leading ladies: "Martha, dear, there are many bonds that will hold us together through eternity: your savings bonds, Liberty bonds, and government bonds."

8. *do*: act or make (verb)
   Do not stick a fork in the toaster.

   *due*: caused by (adjective)
   Due to inclement weather, the underwater basketweaving contest is canceled.

DON'T CONFUSE **THROUGH** WITH **THREW.** THROUGH IS A PREPOSITION; **THREW** IS THE PAST TENSE OF THE VERB "THROW."

9. *reed*: straight stalks of any tall marsh grass
The reeds in the marsh blew in the wind.

*read*: interpret the written word
Reading is fundamental.

10. *dyed*: changed color
Lucille dyed the shoes to match her dress.

*died*: ceased to live
The child was inconsolable when her pet rabbit died.

## PLAY TIME

Tag, you're it. Match each of the following vocabulary words to its meaning.

| | |
|---|---|
| 1. carat | a. dodge; ruse |
| 2. caret | b. quote |
| 3. carrot | c. praise |
| 4. cede | d. sweet |
| 5. seed | e. unit of weight in gemstones |
| 6. cite | f. unlawful |
| 7. sight | g. leave behind |
| 8. site | h. yield |
| 9. complement | i. pass out |
| 10. compliment | j. distinct, separate |
| 11. descent | k. proofreading symbol |
| 12. dissent | l. vision |
| 13. desert | m. go down |
| 14. dessert | n. location; place |
| 15. discreet | o. to draw out |
| 16. discrete | p. veggie |
| 17. elicit | q. disagree |
| 18. illicit | r. kernel |
| 19. faint | s. complete |
| 20. feint | t. tactful |

### ANSWERS

| | |
|---|---|
| 1. e | 11. m |
| 2. k | 12. q |
| 3. p | 13. g |
| 4. h | 14. d |
| 5. r | 15. t |
| 6. b | 16. j |
| 7. l | 17. o |
| 8. n | 18. f |
| 9. s | 19. i |
| 10. c | 20. a |

## Ten More Headaches

Here are ten more. This will be a cakewalk—without the cake, of course.

1. *fare*: the price charged for transporting a passenger
   The bus fare was $1.25.

   *fair*: not biased; moderately large; moderately good
   The teacher, a fair grader, judged the report a fair job and so gave it a "B."

2. *faze*: to stun
   Nothing can faze the king of cool.

   *phase*: a stage
   During an early phase of his life, Richard Nixon worked as a barker for the wheel of chance at the Slippery Gulch Rodeo in Prescott, Arizona.

3. *for*: because
   "History will be kind to me, for I intend to write it" (Winston Churchill).

   *four*: the number 4
   There are four seats left on the bus.

4. *gorilla*: ape
   The gorilla was the prime attraction at the zoo.

   *guerrilla*: soldier
   The guerrilla was armed to the teeth.

5. *grate*: irritate; reduce to small pieces
   To grate on many people's nerves.

   *great*: big, wonderful
   What a great meal you made!

6. *air*: invisible gas that surrounds the earth
   All I need is the air that I breathe and to love you.

*heir*: beneficiary
The heirs contested the will.

7. *here*: in this place
We are here on earth to do good deeds for others. What the others are here for, I don't know.

*hear*: listen
I hear beautiful music coming from the church.

8. *hours:* Sixty-minute periods
Some people stay longer in two hours than others do in a month.

*ours:* belonging to us
It is ours, not yours.

9. *it's*: contraction for it is
It's lonely at the top, but you eat better there.

*its*: possessive pronoun
Madness takes its toll. Please have exact change.

10. *lie*: to tell an untruth
His lie was so transparent that even a child could see through it.

*lie*: be flat
The secret of staying young is to live honestly, eat slowly, and lie down at every opportunity.

## LIFE ON THE EDGE

Why bother cleaning the attic, entertaining your mother-in-law, or getting that pesky root canal when you can supply the homophone for each of these word pairs instead? Write your answer in the space provided.

1. flew
2. heart
3. forward
4. gamble
5. gilt
6. imminent
7. lesson
8. lode
9. mettle
10. residence
11. rote
12. stationary
13. soul
14. suite
15. vale
16. vain and
17. vial
18. whine
19. wear
20. witch

### ANSWERS

| | | | |
|---|---|---|---|
| 1. flue | 6. immanent | 11. wrote | 16. vane, vein |
| 2. hart | 7. lessen | 12. stationery | 17. vile |
| 3. foreword | 8. load | 13. sole | 18. wine |
| 4. gambol | 9. metal | 14. sweet | 19. where |
| 5. guilt | 10. residents | 15. veil | 20. which |

## ALL THE RIGHT MOVES

We're in the home stretch. Stick with me and you'll never confuse tricky word groups again. Here are some additional important vocabulary words that are often confused.

1. *lead*: to guide

   Found in a fortune cookie: Those who lead do not always follow.

   *lead:* bluish-gray metal
   A pound of lead weighs the same as a pound of feathers.

   *led*: past tense of "to lead"
   A Los Angeles man who later said he was "tired of walking," stole a steamroller and led police on a five-mile-per-hour chase until an officer stepped aboard and brought the vehicle to a stop.

2. *meat*: animal flesh

   A louse in the cabbage is better than no meat at all.

   *meet*: encounter; proper
   The friends meet in the park every Sunday to admire the beautiful plantings.

3. *peace:* calm

   Peace:
   Many people are working together for world peace.

   *piece*: section
   The piece of chalk kept breaking, which frustrated the teacher.

4. *plain*: not beautiful; obvious

   The furniture was plain and simply made.

   *plane:* airplane
   Today's planes come equipped with telephones and video games—and they can even fly you long distances for a moderate cost.

5. *presence*: company

   Their presence was about as welcome as hemorrhoids.

   *presents:* gifts

We received some considerate and generous presents for our wedding anniversary.

6. *principal*: main; head of a school
   A principal road in New York City is Fifth Avenue.

   *principle*: rule
   The course covered the principles of engineering.

7. *reed*: straight stalks of any tall marsh grasses
   The marsh was surrounded by tall reeds.

   *read*: interpret the written word
   Can you read a book and listen to music at the same time?

8. *right*: correct
   He who hesitates is probably right.

   *write*: to form letters
   Illiterate? Write today for free help.

9. *their*: belonging to them
   It was their prayer book.

   *they're*: contraction for they are
   They're pleased with the doll.

   *there*: place
   In America there are two classes of travel: first class and with children.

10. *site*: place
   The site must be cleared before the hotel can be built.

   *sight*: vision
   The sight of his daughter in her beautiful bridal gown made him cry.

   *cite*: to quote
   He cited the third line of the ruling to help make his point.

## THE MOMENT OF TRUTH

See, this isn't as difficult as you thought. Now, complete each sentence by choosing the correct vocabulary word.

1. The Friends of the Library was a (nonprophet, nonprofit) organization.
2. A bus carrying five passengers was hit by a car in St. Louis, but by the time the police arrived on the scene, nine pedestrians had boarded the bus and had begun to complain about back (pane, pain).
3. There will be a (reign, rain) dance Friday, (weather, whether) permitting.
4. If you live to the age of 100 years you have it made because very few people die (passed, past) the age of 100.
5. Just remember (you're, your) unique—just like everyone else.
6. (Capitol, Capital) punishment is a hotly debated issue today.
7. There is enough stone in the Great Wall of China (to, too, two) build an eight-foot wall circling the earth at the equator.
8. Most of our future (lays, lies) ahead.
9. Please give this message to (you're, your) mother.
10. In the late 1900s, the man who was shot out of the cannon every day at the Barnum and Bailey Circus decided to quit, for his wife had asked him to find a less risky (weigh, way) of making a living. P. T. Barnum hated to lose a good man, so he sent him a message, "I beg you to reconsider. Men of your caliber are hard to find."
11. Never go to a doctor (who's, whose) office plants have died.
12. In the 1940s, the FCC assigned television's Channel 1 to mobile services (two-way radios in taxicabs, for instance), but did not renumber the other channel assignments. That is why (you're, your) TV set has Channels 2 and up, but no Channel 1.

13. A pedestrian is a parent (whose, who's) child is home from college.

14. Life is (to, too, two) short to stuff a mushroom.

15. I've been on a diet for two (weaks, weeks) and all I've lost is two (weaks, weeks).

16. Warning: Dates on the calendar are closer (then, than) they appear.

17. The man was (borne, born) swiftly to safety.

18. When Hank Aaron was up to bat for the first time in his major league career, the catcher for the opposing team tried to rattle him by saying, "Kid, you're holding the bat all wrong. You should hold it with the label up so you can read it." The young rookie for the Milwaukee Braves, who later went on to become the greatest home-run hitter of all time, replied, "I didn't come up here to (reed, read)."

19. Two (rights, writes) don't make a wrong.

20. If a woman has to choose between catching a fly ball and saving an infant's life, she will choose to save the infant's life without even considering if (there, their, they're) are men on base.

## ANSWERS

| | | | |
|---|---|---|---|
| 1. nonprofit | 6. Capital | 11. whose | 16. than |
| 2. pain | 7. to | 12. your | 17. borne |
| 3. rain, weather | 8. lies | 13. whose | 18. read |
| 4. past | 9. your | 14. too | 19. rights |
| 5. you're | 10. way | 15. weeks, weeks | 20. there |

# CHAPTER 7

# NOW I LIE ME DOWN TO SLEEP:

# COMMONLY CONFUSED WORDS

YOU MUST REMEMBER THIS
Having a powerful command of vocabulary demands that you use words precisely in both verbal and written communication.

ALL THE RIGHT MOVES
Learn to distinguish between commonly confused words by memorizing them, creating mnemonics, or using a dictionary.

## WORDS TO THE WISE

When is it correct to use *accept* and *except*? *Among* and *between*? Have you ever been stumped by the difference between *amount* and *number*? What about *advice* and *advise*? And that's just the tip of the wordberg.

This chapter will help you distinguish between confusing words so you can further polish your command of written and spoken English. Let's start with twelve vocabulary distinctions worth making (or at least being able to make!)

## A DIRTY DOZEN

The following twelve words have driven generations of speakers and writers 'round the bend. No doubt you've been annoyed or aggravated by one or more of them. No more! Read through this section to straighten out once and for all when to use which word.

ABILITY AND CAPACITY

*Ability* means "skill." *Capacity* means "aptitude." Here are two examples:

• After so many years of studying the kazoo, he has the *ability* to play even the most difficult kazoo compositions.

• We all have the *capacity* to love our neighbors (especially if they are not playing the kazoo).

ACCEDE AND EXCEED

*Accede* means "to yield." *Exceed*, in contrast, means "to surpass." Here are two examples:

• I *accede* to your utterly ridiculous demand.

• Don't *exceed* the budget this year.

ACCESS AND EXCESS

*Access* means "the right to use." *Excess* means "surplus, extra, leftover." Here's how they are used:

• We have *access* to the brain from Planet X.

• The *excess* supplies include a hula hoop, a yo-yo, and a truss.

ACCEPT AND EXCEPT

*Accept* means "to receive willingly." It's the verb form of the noun acceptance, "to receive something." The word *except* is a preposition that is related to the noun *exception*. As such, it means "to leave out, to exclude, not include." Check out the following sentences for examples:

• Never *accept* a ride from a stranger.

• We invited everyone—*except* him.

A GREAT DEAL OF CONFUSION IN DISTINGUISHING CERTAIN PAIRS OF WORDS COMES FROM CARELESS OR MUFFLED PRONUNCIATION. IF NECESSARY, SAY THE WORDS IN AN EXAGGERATED WAY TO CONVEY YOUR PRECISE MEANING.

ACCOMPANIED WITH and ACCOMPANIED BY

*Accompanied with* refers to objects. *Accompanied by*, in contrast, refers to people or animals. For instance:

• They were serious shoppers, *accompanied with* charge cards, canvas bags, and water bottles.

• Whenever Big Al paid a visit to our city, he was *accompanied by* his personal cook.

ADEPT AND ADOPT

*Adept* means "skilled." Adopt means "take as your own." Here are two examples:

- As with all cute toddlers, she's *adept* at getting her own way.
- *Adopt* my plan if you have nothing better to suggest.

ADVISE AND ADVICE

*Advise*, a verb, means "to give counsel." Advice, a noun, means "counsel." For example:

- Please *advise* me on what to do.
- Here's some *advice* for you: Never do card tricks for the group you play poker with.

AFFLUENT AND EFFLUENT

*Affluent* means "rich." *Effluent* means "something that flows out." For example:

- You can tell that you're *affluent* if you can buy a yacht and not worry what the gas costs.
- The *effluent* produced by the Widget Company polluted the Kalafachi River.

AGGRAVATE AND ANNOY

Most people use these verbs interchangeably to mean "to bother" or "to make angry," but formal English preserves a useful distinction between the two. *Aggravate* means "to make something worse." *Annoy*, in contrast, means "to bother or harass." For instance:

- It *annoyed* Louis when his wife *aggravated* her allergies by playing with the neighbor's pit bull.

ALLUDE AND ELUDE

*Allude* means "to refer to." Elude, in contrast, means "to escape." Study these examples:

- The joke *alluded* to the creature from the Black Lagoon.
- It's important for one's health and well-being to *elude* fierce creatures at all times.

ALLUSION AND ILLUSION

An *allusion* is a reference to a well-known place, event, person, work of art, or work of literature. Allusions enrich a story or poem by suggesting powerful and exciting comparisons.

An *illusion*, on the other hand, is a misleading appearance or a deception. Here's how the two words are used:

• The entire audience missed the *allusion* to the parable of the loaves and fishes.

• The screenwriter had the illusion that everyone knew the Bible as well as he did.

AMONG AND BETWEEN

This is a number situation. *Among* refers to three or more people, places, or things; *between* refers to two people, places, or things.

• *Among* the three of us, we should be able to cough up enough money to pay this check.

• *Between* the two of us, it's a good deal.

## Tough Love

Got all that down pat? Time to find out. Circle the correct choice in each sentence. Some sentences will have more than one pair of confusing words for you to consider.

1. A doctor can bury his mistakes, but an architect can only (advise, advice) his clients to plant vines.

2. My (affluent, effluent) friend called and said, "I sure missed you at the party last night. I wish you could have joined me." I answered, "I would have, (accept, except) I didn't know how to cancel other plans."

3. It's an (allusion, illusion) that people are paying attention, because no one is listening until you make a mistake.

4. Monday is an (annoying, aggravating) way to spend one-seventh of the week.

5. When two service station attendants in Iona, Michigan, refused to (exceed, accede) to a robber's demands to hand over their (excess, access) cash, the robber threatened to call the police. When the service station attendants still refused to hand over the money, the robber did call the police. He was promptly arrested.

6. You can (accept, except) this as true: For every action, there is an equal and opposite criticism.

7. The severity of the itch is proportional to your (capacity, ability) to reach it.

8. I enjoy doing all dances (accept, except) the Funky Chicken.

9. A conclusion takes shape when you become too (aggravated, annoyed) to keep on thinking.

10. My spiritual advisor gave us good (advice, advise).

11. I have no (allusions, illusions) about dating in my teen years. I was stood up more often than a bowling pin.

12. There was a general agreement (among, between) Jack and Bill on that issue.

13. Shake out the (access, excess) flour before you fry the chicken.

14. The child is always (accompanied by, accompanied with) her nanny.

15. Light-fingered Louie was (adept, adopt) at picking locks.

### ANSWERS

| | | |
|---|---|---|
| 1. advise | 6. accept | 11. illusions |
| 2. affluent, except | 7. ability | 12. between |
| 3. illusion | 8. except | 13. excess |
| 4. annoying | 9. annoyed | 14. accompanied by |
| 5. accede, excess | 10. advice | 15. adept |

## TEN MORE DISTINCTIONS WORTH MAKING

Here are ten more word pairs that are too often abused and misused. Read through the definitions. Then complete the self-test that follows.

AFFECT AND EFFECT

(Get this one down and I promise to spare you lie and lay). Most of the time, *affect* is the verb, implying "influence." For example: "A nice big chunk of imported Swiss chocolate can *affect* your mood." *Effect* is the equivalent noun: "Chocolate has a wonderful *effect* on my mood." There's also the so-called *affect* (watch that noun!) in psychology; all that emotional stuff about a particular psychological state. But don't let it *affect* you too much.

Of course, English isn't that simple. Sometimes *effect* can be a verb. Here's where the situation gets so ugly it can run a bulldog off a meat wagon. When used as a verb, *effect* means "impact and accomplish," as in this example: "I must *effect* my plan to stop eating so much chocolate. By not eating so much chocolate, I have succeeded in *effecting* my plan."

ANXIOUS AND EAGER

Here's one of the famous language bulwarks: You're not *anxious* to spend an evening with old friends, you're *eager* to spend it. (Unless, of course, they are going bungee jumping. Then you are probably *anxious*.) *Anxious* means characterized by an extreme uneasiness of mind, while *eager* means impatient desire.

ASSUME AND PRESUME

When you *presume*, you suppose, perhaps prematurely, that something is true. When you *assume*, in contrast, you take for granted that something is in fact true. *Presume* is thus linked to anticipation. *Assuming* isn't necessarily a great thing, but it's got that in-your-face attitude.

AUTHENTIC AND GENUINE

Something that's *genuine* is the real thing; something that's *authentic* tells the truth about its subject. So, if you spent Monday morning thrilling your co-workers with the details of your weekend scuba diving in St. Lucia when you'd really stayed home and watched reruns of *Gilligan's Island* yet again, your account would not be *authentic*, although you *genuinely* would have wished it to be. Now, if you were eavesdropping on the subway and overheard the story about scuba diving in St. Lucia and repeated the story word for word to your co-workers, that account would be *authentic* (assuming the person in the subway was telling the truth) but not *genuine*, because you'd be passing off someone else's good time as your own.

COMPLEAT AND COMPLETE

This one's a snap; *compleat* is archaic. It's as dated as hot pants and hula hoops. If the world were a fair place, you'd never have to deal with this word again. Unfortunately, the world is not a fair place. For the past few centuries, editors, publishers, and writers have used *compleat* to tart up book titles and boost sales. The first to cotton to this trick was Isaak Walton, back in 1653, with his *The Compleat Angler*, a rumination on fishing and morality. Now we have such noble imitators as *The Compleat Stripper, The Compleat Wyoming Traveler,* and *The Compleat Backpacker (on Ten Cents a Month!)*. No matter how you spell it, the word means "perfectly skilled or equipped."

FARTHER AND FURTHER

This one has kept Greta the Grammarian as busy as a mosquito at a sunbathers' convention. Here's the deal: *farther* means "far"; *further*, "in addition." So, it's *farther* from Long Island to Boca Raton than it is from Long Island to New Jersey. And if you hate malls, you might want to go *farther* away still, to Bora Bora, maybe. Once you've pitched your tent in Bora Bora, no further moves should be necessary. Of course, real estate and English vocabulary being what they are, nothing's that simple. *Further* can be applied to time as well as space; you may have packed up and left Long Island *further* back than you can recall.

FLAUNT AND FLOUT

*Flaunt* means to "parade oneself ostentatiously." If you *flaunt* it, you show it off. Think Pamela Anderson, Cher, and Howard Stern. Now, *flout* means "to be scornful of, to show contempt for," as in: "The government cannot *flout* the will of the people." While both words describe over-the-top behavior, they are virtual opposites.

IMPLY AND INFER

This pair's a matter of perspective, whether you're receiving or sending. You *imply* something in a remark you make to a buddy, who then *infers* something from your words. Therefore, anyone who goes around muttering, "What are you *inferring*?" is committing a grammar faux pas.

ORAL AND AURAL

Something that is *oral* (from the Latin word for "mouth") is spoken, rather than written, whereas something that is *aural* (from the Latin word for "ear") is heard. Of course they're pronounced alike, just to make your life a little more stressful.

SENSUOUS AND SENSUAL

*Sensuous* applies to the delight you get from things that appeal to the senses, such as art, flowers, music, and high-fat ice cream. *Sensual* is linked to erotic pleasures, such as lust.

## Stern Love

You know the drill. Circle the correct choice in each sentence.

1. The humorist Calvin Trillin said, "I'm in favor of liberalizing immigration because of the (affect, effect) it would have on restaurants. I'd let in just about everybody but the English."

2. I am (anxious, eager) to visit the gym after a month off.

3. Your letter allows me to (imply, infer) that you are in good health.

4. A movie mogul once said, "An (oral, aural) contract ain't worth the paper it's written on." And it wasn't.

5. It is (farther, further) from El Paso to Houston than from New York to Detroit.

6. Ms. Universe (flaunted, flouted) her muscles at every opportunity.

7. The saying "getting your goat" comes from an Old English belief that keeping a goat in the barn would have a calming (affect, effect) on the cows, so they would produce more milk.

8. The police decided that the crime warranted (farther, further) investigation.

9. (Flaunting, Flouting) a gag order, the magazine published the unflattering pictures of the actress.

10. Here's a rule you can count on: If you are running late for a flight, the flight will depart from the (furthest, farthest) gate in the terminal.

11. The (affect, effect) of too little sleep is obvious.

12. Lena called off the engagement when she discovered that the twenty-two-carat diamond engagement ring wasn't (genuine, authentic).

13. What did that remark (imply, infer)?

14. Jack made a (complete, compleat) fool of himself when he danced the lambada with the lampshade.

15. We (assumed, presumed) his outlandish story of a fish driving a motorcycle was not true.

## Answers

| | | |
|---|---|---|
| 1. effect | 6. flaunted | 11. effect |
| 2. eager | 7. effect | 12. genuine |
| 3. infer | 8. further | 13. imply |
| 4. oral | 9. Flouting | 14. complete |
| 5. farther | 10. farthest | 15. assumed |

## Top Ten

Here are ten more important word pairs to learn. Learning the difference between the words in each pair can make your everyday vocabulary more precise and powerful. Then you'll speak and write with greater assurance as well as accuracy.

### AMOUNT AND NUMBER

This one's as easy as one, two, three, because it's all about counting. Use the word *amount* when you're describing something that cannot be counted. Use the word *number* when you're describing something that can be counted. For example, you can count kisses, but not love, so the former is measured in a *number* (a large number of kisses); the latter, by *amount* (a great *amount* of love). Here are two more examples:

> **AMOUNT** IS FOLLOWED BY A SINGULAR NOUN, WHILE **NUMBER** IS FOLLOWED BY A PLURAL NOUN.

• Judging by the large *number* of divorces these days, a lot of people who said "I do," didn't.

• The *amount* of peanut butter in the jar is decreasing.

ANGRY AND MAD

In the past, when cars had fins and your fourth-grade teacher was a force to be reckoned with, there was a strong distinction made between these two words. *Angry* was used to describe irritation, while *mad* was reserved for insanity. The distinction is rarely observed today, except by real fussbudgets.

COMPLICATE AND CONFUSE

*Complicate* means "to make more complex," while *confuse* means "to bewilder." Here are two examples:

• Don't *complicate* what should be a simple task.

• Don't *confuse* me. I know it's "Spring ahead, fall back, winter in Miami Beach."

CONTINUAL AND CONTINUOUS

Although both words are adjectives, they have different meanings. *Continual* means "recurring" or "occurring repeatedly." *Continuous* means "uninterrupted in space, time, or sequence." For example:

• Lisa finally saw a doctor about her *continual* headaches.

• Eventually we got used to the *continuous* sound of Junior learning to play the drums.

DESCRIBE AND PRESCRIBE

*Describe* means "to tell what something is like." *Prescribe*, on the other hand, specifies what something must have.

• *Describe* the house for us.

• The law *prescribes* the repairs we must make.

DISINTERESTED AND UNINTERESTED

These words don't mean the same thing, and the distinction between them is worth making to keep your speech and writing clear. *Disinterested* means "neutral" or "uninvolved," while *uninterested* means "bored" or "not interested." For instance:

• The warring couple sought a *disinterested* party to arbitrate their dispute.

• On his days off, the chef was *uninterested* in cooking.

DOMINATE AND DOMINANT

*Dominate* means "to control"; *dominant* means "controlling." Here are two examples:

• The little girl *dominated* her big brother by threatening to tattle on him.

• The gene for brown eyes is *dominant* over the gene for blue eyes.

ELICIT AND ILLICIT

These words have vastly different meanings, even though their pronunciation seems close. *Elicit* means "to draw out" or "bring forth." *Illicit*, in contrast, means "something illegal or forbidden."

• The detective tried to *elicit* a confession from the criminal.

• Even though the criminal was nabbed stealing the jewelry, he refused to admit his *illicit* behavior.

EMIGRATE AND IMMIGRATE

The distinction here is one of geographic direction. *Emigrate* means "to move away from one's country." *Immigrate*, on the other hand, means "to move to another country." Study these examples:

• She *emigrated* from France.

• It's not that easy to adjust when you *immigrate* to a new homeland.

EMINENT, IMMINENT, AND IMMANENT

Here's a pretty pickle: three words that sound alike and are often confused. No more; now they'll all be clear. *Eminent* means "distinguished." *Imminent* means "expected momentarily." *Immanent* means "inborn, inherent." Here are some examples:

• Albert Einstein was an *eminent* professor at Princeton.

• The comet's appearance was *imminent*.

• I have an *immanent* distrust of thunderstorms.

IF YOU FIND THAT YOU FREQUENTLY MISUSE THESE WORDS, YOU MAY WISH TO USE YOUR COMPUTER'S SEARCH-AND-REPLACE FUNCTION TO FIND ALL OCCURRENCES SO THAT YOU CAN EVALUATE EACH ONE.

## Just When You Thought It Was Safe . . .

There's more! Below are six often confused word pairs that you should know. Read through the explanations and examples.

FEWER AND LESS

Use *fewer* for things that can be counted. Use *less* for things that cannot be counted. For example, jokes can be counted, but humor can't be. Here are some additional examples:

- I have *fewer* watches than the salesman on the corner.
- I have less patience than a saint.

GOOD AND WELL

As a modifier, *good* can be used only as an adjective that means "nice." *Well,* in contrast, can be either an adjective or an adverb. Here are some examples:

- You did a *good* job. (adjective)
- You're doing *well.* (adverb)
- I am *well.* (adjective)

"THE DIFFERENCE BETWEEN THE RIGHT WORD AND THE NEARLY RIGHT WORD IS THE SAME AS THAT BETWEEN LIGHTNING AND THE LIGHTNING BUG." (MARK TWAIN)

HANGED AND HUNG

*Hanged* is a past participle used for death sentences; *hung* is used for all other terms meaning "to suspend, dangle, hook." While the distinction is breaking down, purists still observe it, as the following examples show:

- The prisoner was *hanged* for his crimes.
- Portraits of previous directors were *hung* in the boardroom.

HUMAN AND HUMANE

*Human* means "being mortal;" *humane* means "kind, charitable, compassionate." Study these examples:

- Irritating habit: what the endearing little qualities that initially attract two *humans* to each other turn into after a few months together.
- The *humane* society protects the rights of animals.

LEARN AND TEACH

*Learn* means "to receive facts." *Teach* means "to give facts." For instance:

- You *learn* the difference between tricky vocabulary words.
- I *teach* the difference between tricky vocabulary words.

LOOSE AND LOSE

*Loose* can be either an adjective or a verb. As an adjective, *loose* means "not tight, not fastened." As a verb, *loose* means "to untighten, or to let go." *Lose* is a verb that means "to misplace." For example:

- The clasp is *loose*.
- I might *lose* the necklace.

## TEST TIME

You can do this dance, because it's not too tricky. Circle the correct choice in each sentence. Some sentences will have more than one pair of confusing words for you to consider.

1. I am going to speak my mind because I have nothing to (loose, lose.)

2. The (fewer, less) carry-on luggage space available on an aircraft, the (fewer, less) pieces of carry-on luggage passengers will bring aboard.

3. Charles Barkley recently said, "I think that the team that wins the game will win the series. Unless we (loose, lose) game five."

4. I wash everything on the gentle cycle. It's much more (humane, human).

5. The innocent man was (hung, hanged) by an angry mob.

6. The student conductor directs the orchestra surprisingly (well, good).

7. The medical students used computer simulations because they did not want to work on (human, humane) bodies.

8. An (eminent, imminent, immanent) philosopher once said: The trouble with doing something right the first time is that nobody appreciates how difficult it was.

9. The clothes were (hanged, hung) on the line to dry.

10. The (amount, number) of trouble you have is directly proportional to the (amount, number) of trouble you start.

### ANSWERS

| | |
|---|---|
| 1. lose | 6. well |
| 2. less, fewer | 7. human |
| 3. lose | 8. eminent |
| 4. humane | 9. hung |
| 5. hanged | 10. amount, amount |

## IN THE HOME STRETCH

Below are the last ten often confused word pairs. Use a dictionary to help you define each word. (Don't panic; answers follow.)

1. monologue
   soliloquy

2. moral
   morale

3. personal
   personnel

4. precede
   proceed (verb)
   proceeds (noun)

5. quite
   quiet

6. regulate

relegate

7. respectfully

respectively

8. simple

simplistic

9. through

thorough

10. translucent

transparent

## Answers

1. *monologue*: a long talk by a single speaker; *soliloquy*: the act of talking while, or as if, alone
2. *moral:* a lesson, ethical; *morale:* spirit, attitude, state of mind
3. *personal*: what is private, belonging to an individual; *personnel:* staff, employees
4. *precede* (v.): to go before; *proceed* (v.): to continue (Proceed to the exit.); *proceeds* (n.): money (The proceeds go to charity.)
5. *quite*: very; *quiet*: not noisy
6. *regulate:* control; *relegate*: put (usually in a lower rank)
7. *respectfully*: with *respect*; *respectively*: in the stated order
8. *simple:* not complicated; *simplistic:* watered down
9. *through:* in one end and out the other; *thorough:* complete; done without omissions
10. *translucent:* permitting light to pass through, but diffusing it so that objects on the other side cannot be seen clearly; *transparent:* clear, completely see-through

# CHAPTER 8

# THEREBY LIES A TALE:

## LEARN WORD HISTORIES

YOU MUST REMEMBER THIS

Words, like people, have a past, and as with people, some words have more interesting stories than others.

ALL THE RIGHT MOVES

Knowing the history of a word can help you remember that word and make it a part of your daily speech and writing.

People in the Middle Ages rarely tolerated their enemies. As a result, poison sales were brisk. A little dash of poison in a cup of wine or a spicy entree was easily sent down the hatch, dispatching the victim before he or she had a chance to mend fences. Because of the constant danger, wealthy people had a servant standing by whose duty it was to drink from the goblet or sample the dish first. If the servant didn't keel over, the master could eat. The incidence of poisoning was so high in Spain that a special word was created for such precautionary measures: salvo, "to save or protect."

Since the master's food was served on a separate tray, the tray came to be called a salvo as well. As poisoning passed out of general fashion, the term salvo came to be connected with the tray alone, which today we call a salver.

As this story shows, many words have fascinating pasts. In this chapter you'll learn the histories of many useful everyday words. Knowing these stories will make it easier for you to remember what the vocabulary words mean.

## THE NAME GAME

Shakespeare claimed that a rose by any other name would smell as sweet. When it comes to words formed from people's names, however, the word's original purpose sometimes becomes inverted. *Dunce*, for instance, comes from the name of the dazzling thirteenth-century theologian, John Duns Scotus, but today the term *dunce* refers to someone who is decidedly *not* a rocket scientist.

The following ten words have especially interesting backgrounds because they all come from the names and activities of real people. Read through the histories, and then complete the activity that follows.

EPONYMS ARE WORDS FORMED FROM PEOPLE'S NAMES.

BOYCOTT

To *boycott* means to join together in protest as in a strike. The term dates back to 1880. That year, in an attempt to break the death grip of Ireland's absentee landlords, the great Irish leader Charles Stewart Parnell advocated that anyone who took over land from which a tenant had been evicted for nonpayment of rent should be punished "by isolating him from his kind as if he was a leper of old." Parnell's suggestion was applied soon after on the estate of the Earl of Erne. Unable to pay their rents, the tenants tried to secure a lower rate. When the estate manager, Charles Boycott, refused, the tenants not only refused to pay but they also intercepted Boycott's mail and humiliated him in public. This treatment came to be called a *boycott*.

CHAUVINISM

The term *chauvinism* refers to intense and even aggressive nationalism. Nicolas Chauvin, one of Napoleon's most loyal soldiers, couldn't shut up about the glory of his leader and the greatness of his country. He soon became the butt of jokes for his over-the-top nationalism. In 1831, his name was used for a character in a play who worshipped Napoleon. From that play came the term *chauvinism*, which is still in use today.

EPICURE

An *epicure* is an expert in food and other sensual pleasures. The word comes from the Greek philosopher Epicurus (341–270 B.C.), who taught that pleasure from intellectual and spiritual pursuits is the only good.

GERRYMANDER

In 1812, the governor of Massachusetts, Elbridge Gerry, conspired with his party to change the boundaries of the voting districts to enhance his own political power. When a newspaper editor noticed that one such rigged district looked like a salamander, he coined the term *gerrymander* to describe the practice of dividing a state, or any other geographic region, into election districts to give one political party a majority.

MENTOR

In the Odyssey, Mentor is Odysseus's friend. He also tutors Odysseus's son, Telemachus. Today, the term *mentor* means "trusted teacher or guide."

MESMERIZE

In 1775, the Austrian doctor Frederich Anton Mesmer first demonstrated the technique of hypnotism. Today the term *mesmerize* is still used as a synonym for hypnotize, but it has expanded to also mean spellbind or fascinate.

QUISLING

A *quisling* is a traitor—a person who betrays his or her country. It comes from the name of Vidkun Quisling (1887–1945), a Norwegian Army officer turned fascist, who collaborated with the Nazis in World War II.

QUIXOTIC

The word *quixotic* is used to describe lofty but impractical sentiments like those of its namesake, Don Quixote. In 1605, the Spanish writer Miguel Cervantes created the decayed nobleman Don Quixote and his stout servant, Sancho Panza, to parody valiant knights and faithful servants created by previous writers. The elderly Don was the purest embodiment of chivalry; unfortunately, he was also pitifully unaware of his false dreams.

SILHOUETTE

The Seven Years' War and Louis XV's costly mistress, Madame de Pompadour, left France poised on the brink of bankruptcy. By 1759, hoping for a miracle, Madame de Pompadour convinced Louis XV to replace the finance minister with a friend of hers, Etienne de Silhouette. The new appointee immediately instituted a series of stringent reforms. The nobility poked fun at many of the petty regulations, especially the rules calling for coats without folds and snuffboxes made of wood. At the same time, there had also been a revival of the ancient art of tracing the outlines of shadows. Since these shadow profiles replaced many costly paintings, they sneeringly came to be called *a la Silhouette*. Etienne de Silhouette lost his job within the year, but his name has become permanently attached to this art form.

## WHAT'S IN A NAME?

Match each word with its definition. Write the letter of the correct answer in the space provided.

| |  |  |
|---|---|---|
| _____ | 1. quisling | a. an expert in food |
| _____ | 2. mentor | b. profile or outline drawing |
| _____ | 3. mesmerize | c. hypnotize, fascinate |
| _____ | 4. chauvinism | d. traitor |
| _____ | 5. silhouette | e. intense nationalism |
| _____ | 6. quixotic | f. to go on strike |
| _____ | 7. gerrymander | g. rig election districts |
| _____ | 8. epicure | h. trusted teacher or guide |
| _____ | 9. boycott | i. impractical, romantic |

**ANSWERS**

| | |
|---|---|
| 1. d | 6. i |
| 2. h | 7. g |
| 3. c | 8. a |
| 4. e | 9. f |
| 5. b | |

## WORDS OF A FEATHER FLOCK TOGETHER

Animals have contributed their share of words and expressions, too. Here are some examples: *beetle-browed* (an angry, gloomy person), *behemoth* (someone of enormous size), and *chameleon* (a person who changes opinion). Study the following terms for animal groups. They will help you correctly identify masses of animals.

| **Word** | **Animal group** |
|---|---|
| brood | group of chicks, hens |
| covey | family of game birds |

| Word | Animal group |
|---|---|
| drove | group of sheep or oxen |
| flock | group of birds, sheep |
| gaggle | flock of geese |
| gam | group of whales |
| herd | group of animals |
| pride | group of lions |
| school | group of fish |
| shoal | group of fish |
| stable | group of horses |
| swarm | body of bees |

THE WORD **TOPONYM** COMES FROM THE GREEK WORDS **TOPOS** (PLACE) AND **ONOMA** (NAME).

## ARMCHAIR TRAVELER

*Toponyms* are words formed from place names. Let's explore some of these fascinating—and useful—words. Below are ten terms you're likely to encounter in your conversation and writing.

ASCOT

This loose-fitting tie took its name from Ascot Heath, a racetrack near London, the site of famous races.

BIALY

A *bialy* is a chewy, fat roll garnished with a sprinkle of onion flakes. Enterprising bakers in the large Polish city of Bialystock created this yummy sandwich necessity. The *bialy* came to America via Jewish immigrants from Europe.

CHATEAUBRIAND

A mouth-watering thick steak that is split and stuffed with an herb filling. This wonderful creation originated at the family estate of Vicomte François Rene de Chateaubriand, a minor noble who made it through the French Revolution unscathed. The name for the steak came from the name of the estate, located in the Loire Valley in France.

CRAVAT

This term for a tie comes from Croatian soldiers, whom the French called "*Cravate*."

DENIMS

One of the words we use for blue jeans comes from Serge di Nîmes, the city in France where the stiff blue fabric was made.

**JODHPURS,** A TERM FOR RIDING PANTS, ORIGINATED IN JODHPUR, INDIA, WHERE THE BRITISH OVERLORDS WORE THE PANTS AS RIDING BREECHES.

DERBY

Our word for this type of hat hails from the English *derby* races and the man who first wore it, Edward Stanley, the twelfth earl of Derby.

GALOSHES

One term for rubber boots is derived from the sandals worn by the ancient Gauls.

JEANS

This word for a specific kind of pants is from the city where its cloth was made—*Genoa*, Italy. From *Genoa* came *jene*; from *jene*, *jeans*.

MACKINAW

The word we use for a certain type of woolen plaid coat originated in Mackinac Island, currently a resort on Lake Huron, Michigan.

TUXEDO

The word for a man's formal suit comes from Tuxedo, New York. The wealthy and debonair Griswold Lorillard had the tails removed from his formal coat—and a new fashion was born.

## There's Still Time to Change Your Name

Here are ten more useful words that come from the names of real or legendary figures. As you read through these word histories, think about how you would use these words.

The name **canary yellow** comes from the Canary Islands, about sixty miles off the northwest coast of Africa. These islands also gave their name to the popular bird and the bird gave its name to the color, and the slang term for a police informer.

GUILLOTINE

The inventor of the original close shave, Dr. Joseph Guillotin, suggested a beheading machine as a way of ensuring humane executions. In 1791, after Dr. Guillotin had retired from his position in the National Assembly, a man named Antoine Louis actually designed the machine. The guillotine was first used in 1792 to behead a thief; soon after, it was pressed into service during the French Revolution.

MACADAM

As surveyor-general for the roads in Bristol, England, in the early 1800s, John McAdam revolutionized road construction by eliminating the base layer of large stones. We have immortalized the canny Scotsman's clever experiments by using the term *macadam* for a road surface or pavement.

MACKINTOSH

In 1832, Scottish chemist Charles Macintosh discovered that the newfangled substance called "rubber" could be dissolved with the chemical naphtha and painted on cloth to create a waterproof covering. Clothing made with this fabric came to be called *mackintoshes*, or raincoats (as in "Put on your mac, Mac.")

MACHIAVELLIAN

This word comes from the name of the Florentine political philosopher Niccolo Machiavelli (1469–1527) whose masterpiece, *The Prince*, argued that the ends justify the means. They may, but his name has since become a synonym for cunning and deception in the pursuit of power.

MARTINET

In 1660, Colonel Jean Martinet created a drill to whip France's soldiers into shape. Martinet proved to be such an exacting taskmaster that his name came to be applied to any officer intent on maintaining military discipline. In English, a *martinet* is a strict disciplinarian, especially a military one.

ANYONE FACED WITH A SMALL CHILD DETERMINED NOT TO EAT HIS OR HER SPAGHETTI BECAUSE IT "LOOKS LIKE WORMS," BETTER NOT EXPLAIN THE HISTORY OF **VERMICELLI.** IN ITALIAN, THIS TERM FOR SPAGHETTI DOES INDEED MEAN "WORMS." CALL THE STUFF "PASTA" INSTEAD.

NARCISSISM

This term for self-adulation and excessive self-admiration comes from the Greek myth of Narcissus. According to one version of the legend, a Fabio look-alike named Narcissus fell in love with his own image reflected in a pool. Because he was unable to embrace his image, he died from unrequited love.

SIMONY

This term for the buying or selling of a church position comes from Simon the sorcerer, who offered to pay the Apostle Peter to teach him the wondrous cures he had seen Peter perform. Simon did not understand that Peter's feats were miracles rather than magic.

THESPIAN

The term for an actor or actress, comes from a Greek poet named Thespis, who trod the boards around 534 B.C.

ZEPPELIN

The rigid, lighter-than-air flying ship was invented by the Count von Zeppelin in 1900.

## A Break in the Action

To see how you're doing, complete the following exercise by writing the correct definition for each word in the space provided. Select your choices from the definitions in the box. There's one answer for each question, with answers to follow.

| | |
|---|---|
| 1. ____ thespian | a. strict disciplinarian |
| 2. ____ macadam | b. airship |
| 3. ____ mackintosh | c. road surface or pavement |
| 4. ____ simony | d. actor or actress |
| 5. ____ narcissism | e. the buying or selling of ecclesiastical preferments |
| 6. ____ Machiavellian | f. beheading machine |
| 7. ____ martinet | g. self-worship |
| 8. ____ guillotine | h. raincoat |
| 9. ____ zeppelin | i. cunning and deception |

### Answers

1. d. actor or actress
2. c. road surface or pavement
3. h. raincoat
4. e. the buying or selling of ecclesiastical preferments
5. g. self-worship
6. i. cunning and deception
7. a. strict disciplinarian
8. f. beheading machine
9. b. airship

## Let's Get Physical

*Hygiene*, the science of establishing good health, was named for Hygeia, the Greek goddess of health. Hygeia is often shown feeding a snake, a symbol of good health.

How many of these words about the human shape and body parts do you know? Linking the word to its history will help you remember the word and use it correctly.

ADONIS

which means "handsome man," comes from a Greek myth. In the story, Adonis is the heart-throb adored by Aphrodite and Persephone.

GARGANTUAN

which means "enormous," comes from Gargantua, the huge hero of Rabelais's satire, *Gargantua* and *Pantagruel*.

GOLIATH

meaning "large and strong," comes from the biblical giant slain by David.

HERCULEAN

which means "extremely strong," is derived from the mythical hero Hercules.

METHUSELAH

which means "aged," is from the biblical figure Methuselah, who lived 969 years.

SAMSONIAN

meaning "strong," is from the Israelite judge famous for his physical strength.

VENUS

a synonym for a beautiful woman, comes from the Roman goddess of beauty, Venus.

ADAM'S APPLE

a bulge in one's throat, is from the biblical Adam, who ate the apple in the Garden of Eden.

IN THE 1400S, A BAND OF MOSLEMS ESTABLISHED THE OTTOMAN EMPIRE. THE COURT BECAME FAMOUS FOR ITS RICH FURNISHINGS. AMONG THE MOST NOTEWORTHY PIECES WAS A SMALL OVERSTUFFED SEAT, WHICH THE FRENCH DUBBED **OTTOMANE.** THE ENGLISH TRANSLATED THIS TO **OTTOMAN**—THE TERM WE USE TODAY.

IRIS

the colored part of an eye, is from Iris, the Greek goddess of the rainbow.

## FIRST IMPRESSIONS

Below is a list of everyday words for clothing. How many of these articles of clothing can you find in your closet? (P.S.: Each term comes from the name of a person, place, or thing.)

THE BIKINI

an itty-bitty two-piece bathing suit, was created by French fashion designer Louis Reard in 1946. He hoped the abbreviated garment would have the same explosive effect as the atomic bomb detonation that had occurred a few days earlier on the tiny reef of Bikini in the Pacific. Reard's hopes proved prophetic: the bikini shows no signs of declining in popularity.

BLOOMERS

loose underpants, were named for Amelia Bloomer (1818–1894), an American social reformer.

CARDIGAN

a type of sweater, comes from James Brudenell, seventh earl of Cardigan (1797–1868), who wore woolen sweaters while commanding the Light Brigade of the Cavalry during the Crimean War.

KNICKERS

knee-length loose pants, come from "Diedrich Knickerbocker," the fictitious author of *History of New York* by American writer Washington Irving. These pants were a popular fashion at the time of the book's publication in 1809.

DURING PAGAN TIMES IN ENGLAND, ALL THE BONES THAT HAD BEEN COLLECTED DURING THE YEAR WERE BURNED IN A HUGE OUTDOOR FIRE. THE TERM **BONFIRE** CAME TO BE APPLIED TO ANY LARGE FIRE IN THE OPEN AIR.

LEVI'S

is from Levi Strauss, the man who created blue jeans.

A LEOTARD

the close fitting, one-piece garment worn mainly by dancers and acrobats, was named for Jules Leotard, a nineteenth-century French trapeze artist.

PANTS

a common term for trousers, comes from the character Pantaloon in the Commedia dell'Arte who wore big baggy pants.

WELLINGTONS

boots, were named for Arthur Wellington (1769–1852), the Iron Duke. We can only suppose that his feet were always dry, even on the battlefield.

**COFFEE,** DISCOVERED IN KAFFA, ETHIOPIA, WAS FIRST USED AS MEDICINE, THEN AS A STIMULANT BEVERAGE. FROM **KAFFA,** WE GOT **COFFEE.**

## SOUP'S ON

How about a brief snack? Here are some words whose names have interesting histories.

CAJUN

describes the spicy foods characteristic of the Cajun people in Louisiana. The name is a corruption of the French word for the region, Acadia (*dia* is prounced *j*).

CANTALOUPE

a melon, was named for Castle Cantalupo, a papal estate near Vatican City. The melons were grown in the region.

MOCHA

a type of coffee, was named for the Arab seaport of Mukha, in southern Yemen, where the coffee was traded.

HOAGIE

an overstuffed sandwich, hails from Hog Island, south of Philadelphia on the Delaware River. People in this region claim to have invented this sandwich . . . and so does everyone else.

RHUBARB

a celery-like red vegetable, takes its name from the prefix *rha-*, which comes from the ancient name for the Volga River, where the plant grew.

**RHUBARB** IS SLANG FOR "TROUBLE."

STEAK TARTARE

raw chopped meat, hails from the Mongolian and Turkish tribes known as the Tartars or Tatars.

VICHYSSOISE

yummy cold potato and leek soup, is from Vichy, France.

WELSH RABBIT / WELSH RAREBIT

is a bread-and-cheese dish, from Wales, Great Britain.

## "DIAMONDS ARE A GIRL'S BEST FRIEND"

Then we have useful words for precious gems and colors. As you study these words, link them to their histories to make them easier to remember.

**GRAHAM CRACKERS,** NAMED FOR THE FOOD REFORMER SYLVESTER GRAHAM (1794–1851), WERE MEANT TO BE A HEALTH FOOD.

AGATE

a semiprecious quartz, is from the Achates River in Sicily.

ALABASTER

a type of gypsum, is from the town of Alabstron, Egypt. Alabaster is also used as a synonym for "white."

AZURE

a clear blue color, was named for the Latin *lapis lazulum*, meaning "blue stone." Lazuli, in turn, came from the place in Turkistan where the lapis lazuli stones were mined.

CHARTREUSE

a yellow-green color, was named for a liqueur made by the Carthusian monks in Grenoble, France.

COPPER

a reddish metal, took its name from the island of Cyprus.

INDIGO

a deep purple dye, is from India.

MAGENTA

a reddish-purple color, is from a town near Milan, Italy, established by the Roman general Marcus Maxentius.

TURQUOISE

a blue-green gemstone, is from Turkey. *Turkey* became *turquoise* in translation.

## TEST YOURSELF

That was a lot of words you just learned! To help you remember them, complete this simple quiz. Match each word to its definition. Write the letter of the definition in the space provided. You will have definitions left over.

_____1. leotard
_____2. wellingtons
_____3. agate
_____4. magenta
_____5. alabaster
_____6. cardigan
_____7. cantaloupe
_____8. vichyssoise
_____9. indigo
_____10. bloomers
_____11. turquoise
_____12. rhubarb
_____13. chartreuse
_____14. Cajun
_____15. bikini

a. loose underpants
b. spicy food
c. a yellow-green color
d. a melon
e. blue jeans
f. a blue-green colored gemstone
g. potato soup
h. bathing suit
i. vegetable
j. a reddish-purple color
k. knee-length loose pants
l. a semiprecious quartz
m. close-fitting garment
n. raw chopped meat
o. a type of gypsum; white
p. a deep-purple dye
q. a type of sweater
r. a type of coffee
s. sandwich
t. boots

### ANSWERS

| | | |
|---|---|---|
| 1. m | 6. q | 11. f |
| 2. t | 7. d | 12. i |
| 3. l | 8. g | 13. c |
| 4. j | 9. p | 14. b |
| 5. o | 10. a | 15. h |

# CHAPTER 9

# LEND ME A WORD:

## WORDS FROM OTHER LANGUAGES

> YOU MUST REMEMBER THIS
>
> Many of our most useful everyday words come from other languages, including French, Spanish, Italian, Celtic (Irish), Arabic, Indian, and Iranian. Other useful words were newly minted.
>
> ALL THE RIGHT MOVES
>
> Knowing a word's country of origin can help you figure out what it means and how it is used.

China is the most populous country on earth, boasting more than 1 billion citizens. Japan, in contrast, has only about 125 million people—but it does have some great sushi. France has one television for every two people, 63 airports, and a ton of perfume. Spain? More than 895,000 metric tons of fish were caught there in 1996.

What do all these countries have in common? In addition to people, perfume, and pike, they have all given us loads of handy words. English has embraced words from heaps of other languages and dialects, near and far, ancient and modern. And when we can't find a word that we need, we just invent one. You'll be surprised to learn how many of these words you've been using everyday originated in other languages.

One of the most effective ways to stretch your vocabulary is by learning a word's origins. This helps you link related words, so you can figure out the meaning and usage of many other commonplace words that have entered English from other countries. The following three suggestions can help you make these foreign-born words part of your daily vocabulary:

1. Jot down unfamiliar words that you hear or read.

2. Look up the word in a dictionary to find out its origin. Note the foreign language the word comes from.

3. Group related words. For example, put all the words from French together. This will make it easier for you to see how the words are similar.

THREE OUT OF FOUR WORDS IN THE ENGLISH DICTIONARY ARE FOREIGN BORN.

In this chapter, you'll learn some words from other languages that you can use daily to express yourself more clearly in print and writing. So fasten your seat belt, extinguish all smoking materials, and place your tray table in the upright position as we begin our journey to the different countries where important English words were born.

WE CAN BORROW SUGAR FROM A NEIGHBOR ONLY BECAUSE ENGLISH BORROWED THE WORD "SUGAR" FROM SANSKRIT CENTURIES AGO.

## WORDS WE'VE IMPORTED

English has welcomed an astonishing number of foreign words. Take this simple quiz to see what I mean. Match each of the following words with its native language. Write the letter of the correct choice in the blank by the number.

| | | |
|---|---|---|
| ____ | 1. hacienda | a. French |
| ____ | 2. borscht | b. Celtic (Irish) |
| ____ | 3. gravel | c. Arabic |
| ____ | 4. charlatan | d. Italian |
| ____ | 5. juggernaut | e. Spanish |
| ____ | 6. admiral | f. India |
| ____ | 7. domo | g. Yiddish |
| ____ | 8. crescendo | h. a word that was just invented! |

### ANSWERS

| | |
|---|---|
| 1. e | 5. f |
| 2. g | 6. c |
| 3. c | 7. h |
| 4. a | 8. d |

## Invade and See the World

For ages, fair-haired hunky sailors from North Germany roamed the high seas at will. Around A.D. 449, these Anglo-Saxon mariners sailed across the North Sea and landed in a place then called Britannia. That explains why English is a Germanic language at heart.

In 1066, the Normans conquered England and the Norman language, French, became the official tongue. (Latin was still used in church and school.) William the Conqueror's victory added a new layer of language as well as a new government and some decent food.

After the Normans, England was invaded by culture rather than by warriors. As the English traded with their neighbors on the Continent, they acquired words as well as goods from: France, Spain, Italy, Germany, Poland, Ireland, the Arab states, India, and Iran.

## Ooo La La! English Words from French

From the French, we've imported some great perfumes, paté, and words. For example, we use many French words to describe people, including their personalities, occupations, and personal habits. Some are adjectives, like *naive*, which means "unsophisticated, simple." Others are nouns, such as *ingenue*, which means "a frank or artless young woman."

How many French words do you use regularly? How many have you heard or read and wished you understood? On the following chart, underline each word from French that would help you speak and write with greater clarity and precision.

| **Word** | **Meaning** |
|---|---|
| bon mot | clever saying |
| bourgeois | middle class |
| charlatan | faker, quack |
| faux pas | social blunder |
| gauche | socially inept |
| genteel | elegant, refined |
| nonchalance | indifference |
| rapport | harmony, accord |
| repartee | witty talk |
| raconteur | expert storyteller |

A **BON VIVANT** IS A PERSON WHO LIVES WELL. CAVIAR, ANYONE?

One effective way to enhance your vocabulary is to arrange the words into related groups. Giving the words a common frame of reference makes them easier to memorize, recall, and use correctly. The following ten words from French concern food and cooking. To reinforce your knowledge, try to use each word in a sentence.

## Soup's On

| Word | Meaning |
|---|---|
| aspic | gelatin made with meat or fish stock |
| béchamel | white sauce often seasoned with nutmeg |
| bouillon | broth or stock |
| casserole | a baking dish or a one-meal dish |
| compote | stewed fruit |
| croquette | patty of meat, fish, or vegetables covered in bread crumbs and fried |
| cuisine | style of cooking |
| fricassee | stewed meat served in a white sauce |
| meringue | whipped egg whites sweetened with sugar and baked to light brown |
| ragout | highly-seasoned stew of meat, fish, or vegetables |

## Kick Up Your Heels

The following words from French describe entertainment. See how many of these ten diverting words you know.

| Word | Meaning |
|---|---|
| arabesque | fanciful, interlaced patterns |
| burlesque | ludicrous parody |
| cabaret | dinner show |
| cotillion | complex, formal dance; a formal ball |
| croupier | the attendant at a gaming table |
| marquee | sign used outside a theater |
| pirouette | to whirl on one foot |
| roulette | game of chance |
| troubadour | wandering singer |
| vaudeville | variety show consisting of light, amusing pieces |

ASK YOUR **PAL** (ROMANY) TO GO TO THE **OPERA** (ITALIAN) AND SHE MAY PREFER TO GO HUNTING IN THE **BOONDOCKS** (TAGALOG), PLAY **POLO** (TIBETAN), OR VISIT THE **ZOO** (GREEK).

## Build a Better Mousetrap

Try to link each of the following words borrowed from the French with a mental picture of the structure. That will make the words easier to remember and use correctly.

| Word | Meaning |
|---|---|
| bas-relief | sculpture in which the figures project slightly from the background |
| boulevard | broad avenue in a city, often tree-lined |
| bureau | office, desk |
| canteen | small container used to hold liquid |
| chaise | light, open carriage |
| chateau | castle |
| concierge | doorman |
| epergne | ornamental dish for holding fruit or flowers |
| escritoire | writing desk |
| facade | front of a building |
| mansard | roof with two slopes at different levels |
| salon | drawing room in a large house; a shop related to fashion |

Each of these words from French describes conflict: **espionage, saboteur,** and **melee.** How many of these words do you know?

## Olé! English Words from Spanish

Spanish words have entered English not only from Spain but also from many other Spanish-speaking places in the world, including Mexico, Puerto Rico, Central America, and South America.

Here are some English words from Spanish we use to describe places and building materials. See if you can define each word. Feel free to use a dictionary.

1. adobe ________________
2. arroyo ________________
3. canyon ________________
4. hacienda ________________
5. patio ________________
6. pueblo ________________

7. rancho

8. sierra

## Answers

How many of these definitions did you get?

1. sun-dried brick
2. gulch
3. valley with steep sides
4. landed estate
5. courtyard
6. adobe houses
7. hut that shelters travelers
8. chain of hills or mountains

## Getting to Know You

Here are five words from Spanish that describe people. How many of these words would you use to describe *your* friends and family?

| **Word** | **Meaning** |
|---|---|
| bravado | bluster |
| desperado | bold, reckless criminal |
| hombre | man |
| picaroon | pirate |
| renegade | deserter |

HERE ARE SOME WORDS FROM SPANISH WE USE FOR FOODS: **ANCHOVY, AVOCADO, BANANA, BARBECUE, CARAMEL, CHILI CON CARNE, DORADO, PIMENTO, POMPANO, POTATO, TAMALE, TORTILLA,** AND **VANILLA.**

## To Arms!

The following words borrowed from the Spanish are all associated with military matters. Learn these words by reading the list over several times. Every few minutes, look up from your reading and try to recall each word.

| **Word** | **Meaning** |
|---|---|
| armada | a fleet of warships |
| comrade | fellow soldier |

| Word | Meaning |
|---|---|
| embargo | restricting commerce |
| flotilla | group of ships |
| guerrilla | radical, independent soldier |
| intransigent | inflexible |
| junta | ruling group |
| presidio | fort, garrison town |

## GIDDYAP!

Saddle up, partner, because the following words from Spanish are all associated with ranching. You'll find many of these words appear in novels about the West. See how many you can define. Answers follow.

1. bronco
2. caballero
3. chaparral
4. corral
5. lariat
6. lasso
7. mustang
8. rodeo
9. stampede
10. vaquero

### ANSWERS

1. untamed horse
2. Spanish gentleman, a horseman
3. dense thicket of oaks
4. enclosed pen for horses
5. rope used for catching horses
6. long, noosed rope used for catching horses
7. small, hardy horse
8. public showing of cowboy skills
9. sudden, frenzied rush of cattle
10. cowboy or herdsman

## La Dolce Vita: English Words from Italian

Next to Latin and French, Italian has provided the most words that we use frequently in English. Many of our imported Italian words deal with art, music, and literature, but other areas have been flavored by Italian as well.

How many of these made-in-Italy words do you know? Write **T** if the definition is true; write **F** if it is false.

| | | |
|---|---|---|
| _____ | 1. allegro | pale yellow fruit |
| _____ | 2. bandit | robber |
| _____ | 3. barrack | building for lodging soldiers |
| _____ | 4. bravo | well done, good |
| _____ | 5. citadel | fortress |
| _____ | 6. fracas | uproar |
| _____ | 7. impresario | someone who organizes or manages public entertainment |
| _____ | 8. legato | a type of footwear |
| _____ | 9. maestro | a famous conductor |
| _____ | 10. vendetta | private, vengeful feud |

### Answers

Only 1 and 8 are false; all the rest are true. *Allegro* means "at a brisk or rapid pace;" *legato* means "at a smooth and connected pace." Both terms are used to describe the pace of a musical composition.

## Play On, Maestro!

The following English words from Italian help us name musical people, places, and things. To help you remember the words after you learn them, you may wish to write each one on an index card, with the definition on the back.

| **Word** | **Meaning** |
|---|---|
| bravo | well done, good |
| crescendo | a gradual increase in force, volume, or loudness |
| duet | a musical composition for two voices or instruments |
| finale | the last piece, division, or movement in musical composition or dance |

| Word | Meaning |
|---|---|
| impresario | a person who organizes or manages public entertainment |
| libretto | the text of a long musical piece, such as an opera |
| maestro | a famous conductor |
| quartet | a group of four musicians |
| soprano | the highest singing voice |
| tarantella | a rapid, whirling dance |

## BUILDING BLOCKS

Travelers flock to Italy for many reasons: the rich culture, fine food, and stunning buildings—especially those buildings! Who wouldn't like to visit the Roman Coliseum, the Sistine Chapel, the Vatican, and the Leaning Tower of Pisa? English has seized the following words from Italian to describe different aspects of architecture; see how many of these words about buildings you know.

| Word | Meaning |
|---|---|
| arcade | arched passageway, shops |
| catacomb | tomb |
| colonnade | columns |
| cornice | molding |
| cupola | dome |
| frieze | decorative band |
| grotto | cave |
| mezzanine | lowest balcony |
| portico | porch |
| rotunda | round building |

THE ITALIAN WORDS **PRIMA DONNA** (LITERALLY, "FIRST WOMAN") REFER TO THE PRINCIPAL FEMALE SINGER IN AN OPERA OR CONCERT COMPANY. PRIMA DONNAS ARE NOTORIOUS FOR THEIR UNWILLINGNESS TO SHARE THE STAGE, AND SO WE OFTEN USE THE TERM **PRIMA DONNA** TO DESCRIBE A TEMPERAMENTAL SHOW-OFF.

## WAR AND PEACE

Words enter English (as well as other languages) in many ways. Often, the new borrowing fills a language gap by describing an event or person. The following English words originated in Italy. Each describes some aspect of the military or a war-like conflict:

| Word | Meaning |
|---|---|
| bandit | a robber |
| barrack | a building for lodging soldiers |
| battalion | an army in battle array |
| cavalier | a horseman |
| citadel | a fortress |
| fracas | uproar |
| salvo | a round of artillery |
| stiletto | a short dagger with a slender blade |
| vendetta | a private feud |

## TRADE TIME

Countries trade more than goods and services. Words are also passed along with the transaction. Below are some English words from Italian about commerce for you to explore.

| Word | Meaning |
|---|---|
| carat | a unit of weight in gemstones |
| contraband | smuggled goods |
| majolica | earthenware |
| mercantile | pertaining to trade |
| parmesan | a type of cheese |
| porcelain | fine china |

A **BAGEL** IS A CHEWY ROLL WITH A HOLE IN THE MIDDLE. ALSO CALLED AN "ALLIGATOR TEETHING RING," THIS TREAT HAS BECOME UBIQUITOUS THROUGHOUT AMERICA, THANKS TO MASS MARKETING.

## ENGLISH WORDS FROM YIDDISH

Some people claim that Yiddish is a dying language. If that's so, why have so many of its words become commonplace in daily usage? These words appear in books, on television, and in conversation.

Here are ten Yiddish words that pertain to food. See how many of these foods you want to add to *your* shopping list.

| Word | Meaning |
|---|---|
| blintzes | pancake folded around a cheese or fruit filling |

| Word | Meaning |
|---|---|
| borscht | beet soup |
| challah | soft egg bread |
| gefilte fish | fish cakes |
| hamantash | triangle-shaped jam-filled cookies |
| knaydl | dumpling |
| knish | little filled dumplings |
| kreplach | a dumpling, like Italian ravioli |
| lox | smoked salmon |
| matzoth | unleavened bread |

## English Words from Irish (Celtic)

Another fertile source of English words is Celtic. Pronounced with a hard "C," these Celts have added great richness to our language, as you will shortly discover. See how many of the following ten words from Celtic you know and use.

| Word | Meaning |
|---|---|
| clan | group of families or households |
| crag | steep, rugged rock |
| gull | aquatic bird; to cheat or swindle |
| javelin | light spear, usually thrown by hand |
| loch | lake |
| menhir | upright monumental stone, found chiefly in Cornwall |
| quay | dock |
| skein | length of yarn wound in coil |
| toque | twisted narrow band; something that creates tension |
| Tory | member of the Conservative Party in England |

Below are some other useful everyday words that have come into English from our Irish immigrants. Check your definitions and pronunciation in a dictionary.

| | |
|---|---|
| shamrock | blarney |
| banshee | leprechaun |
| galore | plaid |
| brogue | ptarmigan |
| truant | colleen |

## English Words from the Arabic, Indian, and Iranian

English has also adopted important everyday vocabulary words from the Arab states, India, and Iran. Many of these words were introduced to English by traders. Match each of the following words with its meaning. Write the letter of the correct choice in the blank by the number.

| | | |
|---|---|---|
| _____ | 1. albacore | a. gazelle, sprite |
| _____ | 2. alchemy | b. wild cat |
| _____ | 3. ariel | c. wealthy, powerful person |
| _____ | 4. bandanna | d. wise leader |
| _____ | 5. camphor | e. a dye |
| _____ | 6. garble | f. expert, authority |
| _____ | 7. guru | g. pungent yellow spice |
| _____ | 8. henna | h. scarf |
| _____ | 9. karma | i. herb |
| _____ | 10. nabob | j. strong-smelling analgesic |
| _____ | 11. nirvana | k. heaven, freedom |
| _____ | 12. panther | l. mix up |
| _____ | 13. pundit | m. fate |
| _____ | 14. saffron | n. fish |
| _____ | 15. tarragon | o. magic |

### Answers

| | | |
|---|---|---|
| 1. n | 6. l | 11. k |
| 2. o | 7. d | 12. b |
| 3. a | 8. e | 13. f |
| 4. h | 9. m | 14. g |
| 5. j | 10. c | 15. i |

## More! More!

Below are additional words from Arabic. Use a dictionary to define any unfamiliar words. See how many of these words you use.

| | |
|---|---|
| algorithm | monsoon |
| almanac | sumac |

| | |
|---|---|
| alkali | nadir |
| elixir | carafe |
| arsenal | zenith |

## More Than the Taj Mahal

Below are a group of words from different Indian dialects. Study the words and their definitions so you can use them properly.

| **Word** | **Meaning** |
|---|---|
| panther | wild cat |
| ginger | spice |
| nirvana | heaven, freedom |
| karma | fate |
| pundit | expert, authority |
| bandanna | scarf |
| myna | bird |
| nabob | wealthy, powerful person |
| chutney | sweet and sour sauce |
| guru | wise leader |

DID YOU KNOW THAT WE ALSO GOT THE WORDS **SHAMPOO** AND **LOOT** FROM INDIAN DIALECTS?

## Brave New Words: Created Words

Our language, like the weather, is a popular topic: everybody's got something to say about it. And like the weather, where there's language, there is also change. What can you do if the English language doesn't have the word you need? Just make it up!

President Thomas Jefferson created the word *belittle;* writer Lewis Carroll, the word *chortle*. Other words we created in the past include *groundhog*, *lightning rod*, and *seaboard*. Shakespeare created 10 percent of the words he used—and look where it got him.

A **NEOLOGISM** IS THE TERM FOR A NEWLY MINTED WORD.

Besides, how do you think we came up with all those new computer terms like *byte*, *RAM*, and *ROM*? Coining words is what helps create the vitality of the language.

Does the concept of coining words make you uncomfortable? OK, then take an existing word and adapt it to your needs. The catch: enough people have to agree with you to make the word into a meaningful sound bite. (Notice how I sneaked in that new coinage "sound bite"? How old do you think *that* term is?)

Here are ten newly coined words that may or may not make the cut to commonly accepted usage. Cast your vote early and often. Your use of these words will determine which ones eventually make it into the major league dictionaries.

FREEMAN (noun)

a unit that measures the amount of plagiarism in a text. The word was coined in 1987 during a successful copyright-infringement suit.

MAD-DOG (verb)

to stare at someone as though to spark a fight. It seems likely that the shift in meaning from a noun (a rabid dog) to a verb is the work of Los Angeles gangs.

**A SUPER TWIN** IS ANY CHILD BORN OF A MULTIPLE BIRTH OF THREE OR MORE.

RUG-RANKING (noun)

a policy that assigns secretarial status and pay on the basis of the boss's status rather than on secretarial skills required for the job. The earliest known usage of this word was 1990.

URBAN YOGA (noun)

a new form of exercise, also known as "power yoga." This coinage is similar to words like *urban guerrilla*, *urban homesteading*, *urban renewal*, and *urban sprawl*.

**SPUTNIK** APPEARED IN THE DICTIONARY FASTER THAN ANY OTHER WORD IN HISTORY, SAYS DAVID BARNHART, EDITOR OF **THE BARNHART DICTIONARY**. IN 1957, SIX HOURS AFTER THE RUSSIAN SATELLITE WAS LAUNCHED, BARNHART'S FATHER STOPPED THE PRESSES AND ADDED THE WORD TO THE DICTIONARY.

ATTACK FAX

to aggressively fax an opponent.

DOMO

a downwardly mobile professional.

GHOST RIDER

a person who fakes an injury at the scene of an accident in which he or she wasn't involved, hoping to profit from any lawsuits. *Add-on* and *jump-on* are other new terms for the same scam.

GOING POSTAL

having a messy, violent breakdown. The term comes from several incidents involving postal workers becoming deranged and shooting people while still on duty.

STARTER MARRIAGE

a first marriage.

WHINNER

a person who whines even when he or she wins.

**PARKMAN** IS THE NEW WORD FOR THE ENERGY FORCE THAT EXPLAINS WHY SOME PEOPLE ALWAYS SEEM TO FIND A GOOD PARKING SPACE—NO MATTER WHAT THE TIME OR PLACE.

# CHAPTER 10

# LEARN THE LINGO: PROFESSIONAL WORDS

YOU MUST REMEMBER THIS

The professions of computer technology, engineering, law, and medicine, greatly affect your daily life.

ALL THE RIGHT MOVES

Knowing words from these professions is essential in today's complex world.

You know that each profession has its own special words, called *jargon*. For example, we call a mistake in a computer program a "bug," but you know that a computer "bug" is not the same as the insect you swatted yesterday. That's because the computer term "bug," as with many specialized terms, has become part of our everyday vocabulary. Educated people, like you, know how important it is to understand these terms to keep pace with a fast-changing world—especially on the eve of the twenty-first century. Let's start by looking at some important computer terms that have entered everyday vocabulary.

## BYTE ME

It is a truth universally acknowledged that computers are used by almost one-third of all Americans at work or at home. In just a decade, the percentage of people age eighteen or older who use a computer has doubled, from 18 percent in 1984 to 36 percent in 1994 (the latest year for which figures are available). This percentage is sure to rise faster than a quark in a particle accelerator, since 59 percent of children between the ages of three and seventeen used computers in 1994. In 1996, more than $11,000,000 worth of computer hardware was sold. That makes for a lot of happy bean counters, investors, and consumers.

These statistics also show that it's essential to know everyday computer terms. So, here are ten important words that have entered daily speech and writing from computer technology:

MANY MOUSE DEVICES ARE NOW BUILT INTO KEYBOARDS AS BUTTONS OR ROLLING BALLS.

| Term | Meaning |
|---|---|
| DISK | flexible plastic wafer used to store information; also called floppy disk although today's disks are as firm as Atilla the Hun's resolve |
| DISK DRIVE | where you insert a floppy disk or the hard disk |
| DOS | disk operating system, a program for storing information, contains the instructions for how your computer should operate |
| LAPTOP | small, lightweight, portable battery-powered notebook computer with a thin, flat, liquid crystal display screen |
| MEMORY | term for storage of information |
| MENU | collection of command options for performing actions in a program |
| MODEM | device that enables computers to connect and transfer data over phone lines by converting digital signals into analog signals |
| MOUSE | pointing device that controls the cursor movement on the screen |
| PC | personal computer |

**HARDWARE** IS THE TERM FOR THE PHYSICAL AND MECHANICAL COMPONENTS OF A COMPUTER SYSTEM—THE ELECTRONIC CIRCUITRY, CHIPS, SCREENS, DISK DRIVES, KEYBOARDS, AND PRINTERS.

| | |
|---|---|
| VIRUS | undesirable computer programs that are designed to be transmitted unobserved by a computer user in order to damage data |

## DRIVE ON THE INFORMATION SUPERHIGHWAY

Have you "driven" on the information superhighway yet? The "information superhighway"—the *Internet*—links people through computer terminals and telephone lines to a web of software and networks in *cyberspace*. *Cyberspace* is a series of computer networks and bulletin boards in which on-line communication takes place. According to current estimates, about 15 million people in the United States and 25 million people around the world regularly "surf the net," as accessing information on the *Internet* is called.

> **SOFTWARE** IS THE TERM FOR THE COMPUTER PROGRAMS, WHICH ARE THE PRECISE SERIES OF INSTRUCTIONS WRITTEN IN COMPUTER LANGUAGE THAT TELL THE COMPUTER WHAT TO DO AND HOW TO DO IT.

Since computers burst on the scene less than a generation ago, they have contributed a tremendous number of words that we use daily. Here are ten more that it's important to know because they all relate to word processing.

| **Term** | **Meaning** |
|---|---|
| COPY | reproduce the material in an additional spot in the document or onto a disk |
| CURSOR | the pulsing spot on the screen that signals where material can be typed |
| CUT AND PASTE | move text to a different place in a document |
| FILE | a document you have created and saved |
| HARD COPY | a paper copy of your document |
| INSERT | place an object such as a graphics file into a document |
| SAVE | record on disk or hard drive |

| Term | Meaning |
|---|---|
| SCROLL | move up and down the document on screen |
| SELECT | mark off a section on the screen |
| TEXT | the letters, numbers, punctuation, and symbols you type in a document |

## OPEN THE WINDOWS

Match each of the following computer terms with its meaning. Write the letter of the correct choice in the blank by the number.

| | Term | Meaning |
|---|---|---|
| ____ | 1. DOS | a. notebook computer |
| ____ | 2. PC | b. highlight a section on the screen |
| ____ | 3. cursor | c. a paper copy of your document |
| ____ | 4. mouse | d. flexible plastic wafer |
| ____ | 5. select | e. term for storage of information |
| ____ | 6. copy | f. reproduce the material |
| ____ | 7. cut and paste | g. program for storing information |
| ____ | 8. file | h. controls cursor |
| ____ | 9. virus | i. damaging computer programs |
| ____ | 10. hard copy | j. to record on disk |
| ____ | 11. memory | k. move up and down the document on screen |
| ____ | 12. laptop | l. document you created and saved |
| ____ | 13. scroll | m. to move text |
| ____ | 14. save | n. pulsing spot on the screen |
| ____ | 15. disk | o. personal computer |

### ANSWERS

| | | |
|---|---|---|
| 1. g | 6. f | 11. e |
| 2. o | 7. m | 12. a |
| 3. n | 8. l | 13. k |
| 4. h | 9. i | 14. j |
| 5. b | 10. c | 15. d |

A KNOWLEDGE OF ROOTS, SUFFIXES, AND PREFIXES CAN BE ESPECIALLY HELPFUL WHEN YOU DECODE PROFESSIONAL, TECHNICAL, AND ACADEMIC TERMS, WITH THEIR HEAVY RELIANCE ON LATIN AND GREEK SOURCES. WHY NOT REVIEW CHAPTERS 2, 3, AND 4 NOW?

## LEGAL BEAGLES

Below are ten terms from the legal profession that have entered general usage. How many of these words have you heard or read and wished you understood? On the following chart, circle each word that you know.

| **Word** | **Meaning** |
|---|---|
| accuse | to charge someone with a crime |
| acquit | to free from blame |
| commute | reduce a charge or punishment |
| culpability | the blame |
| defendant | person being accused or sued |
| hearsay | evidence based on someone else's statements |
| jurisdiction | legal power to hear and decide cases |
| litigation | lawsuit |
| plaintiff | person who brings a lawsuit |
| subpoena | written order commanding a person to testify in court |

WHAT'S IN AN "E"? A LOT, WHEN IT COMES TO CASES AND CAKES. TO A LAWYER, A **TORT** IS A CIVIL WRONG FOR WHICH THE INJURED PARTY IS ENTITLED TO COMPENSATION. TO A BAKER, A **TORTE** IS A RICH CAKE—ESPECIALLY ONE THAT CONTAINS LITTLE OR NO FLOUR.

## VAULT THE BAR

Here are some legal words we use to describe specific types of crimes. See if you can deduce what crime each is guilty of. Answers follow.

1. assault
2. battery
3. collusion
4. embezzlement
5. extortion
6. larceny
7. perjury
8. slander
9. libel

### ANSWERS

1. an attempt or threat to do violence to another person
2. an unlawful attack on another person by touching, beating, and so on in an offensive manner
3. a secret agreement for fraudulent purposes; conspiracy
4. misappropriation or theft of money
5. the wrongful seizure of a person's money or property with his consent but by the use of violence or threat
6. robbery, theft
7. uttering false statements while under oath in court
8. defamation; false and malicious oral statements
9. oral or written defamation that conveys an unjustly unfavorable impression

## TRUTH OR CONSEQUENCES

In the space provided, write **T** if the definition is true or **F** if it is false.

_______ 1. accuse: to charge someone with a crime
_______ 2. acquit: to free from blame
_______ 3. battery: attack

______ 4. collusion: conspiracy
______ 5. commute: reduce a charge or punishment
______ 6. culpability: the blame
______ 7. defendant: person being accused or sued
______ 8. embezzlement: theft of money
______ 9. extortion: defamation
______ 10. hearsay: not neccessarily true
______ 11. jurisdiction: a written order directing a person to appear in court
______ 12. larceny: slander
______ 13. litigation: lawsuit
______ 14. plaintiff: person who brings a lawsuit
______ 15. subpoena: order to appear in court

### ANSWERS

|  |  |  |
|---|---|---|
| 1. T | 6. T | 11. F |
| 2. T | 7. T | 12. F |
| 3. T | 8. T | 13. T |
| 4. T | 9. F | 14. T |
| 5. T | 10. T | 15. T |

THE LATIN ROOT **CORP** MEANS "BODY." A NUMBER OF LEGAL WORDS COME FROM THIS ROOT, INCLUDING THE PHRASES **A WRIT OF HABEAS CORPUS** (LITERALLY, "PRODUCE THE BODY") AND **CORPUS DELICTI** ("BODY OF THE CRIME").

## RX: MEDICAL WORDS

Daily, we use an amazing number of words that originated in the healing professions. Take the following simple quiz to see what I mean. Match each of the following words that describe a medical condition with its meaning. Write the letter of the correct choice in the blank by the number. Answers follow.

| | |
|---|---|
| ____1. metastasis | a. catching |
| ____2. psychosis | b. poisonous |
| ____3. amnesia | c. cancerous |
| ____4. benign | d. disease moves to another part of the body |
| ____5. tumor | e. identification of illness |
| ____6. comatose | f. unconscious |
| ____7. lesion | g. skin rash |
| ____8. toxic | h. harmless |
| ____9. atrophy | i. gum swelling |
| ____10. dermatitis | j. a detachment from reality |
| ____11. malignant | k. very bad headache |
| ____12. gingivitis | l. injury, wound |
| ____13. migraine | m. memory loss |
| ____14. diagnosis | n. shrivel |
| ____15. contagious | o. mass |

A **CARDIOLOGIST** IS A DOCTOR WHO SPECIALIZES IN HEART CONDITIONS; AN **EPIDEMIOLOGIST** SPECIALIZES IN INFECTIOUS DISEASES.

### ANSWERS

| | | | | |
|---|---|---|---|---|
| 1. d | 4. h | 7. l | 10. g | 13. k |
| 2. j | 5. o | 8. b | 11. c | 14. e |
| 3. m | 6. f | 9. n | 12. i | 15. a |

## CURE-ALL

Here are ten more medical terms that well-informed health-care consumers should know. Read the words and the definitions several times until you have them fixed in your mind.

| **Word** | **Meaning** |
|---|---|
| alopecia | hair loss |
| antiseptic | something that kills germs |
| bulimia | serious eating disorder |
| congenital | inborn, inherited |
| hematoma | swelling |
| intravenous | substance administered into the veins |
| myopia | near-sightedness |

| Word | Meaning |
|---|---|
| neuralgia | nerve pain |
| remission | disappearance of disease symptoms |
| rubella | type of measles |

## Check-up Time

The doctor is in! Since you're now the word specialist, write a definition for each of the following medical terms. Suggested answers follow.

1. lesion
2. remission
3. migraine
4. congenital
5. contagious
6. rubella
7. psychosis
8. antiseptic
9. bulimia
10. dermatitis

### Answers

1. injury, wound
2. disappearance of disease symptoms
3. severe headache
4. inborn, inherited
5. catching
6. type of measles
7. a detachment from reality
8. something that kills germs
9. eating disorder
10. skin condition

WHAT TYPE OF DOCTOR SHOULD YOU SEE IF YOU HAVE SOMETHING WRONG WITH YOUR GUMS? A **PERIODONTIST** IS A GUM SPECIALIST.

## CONCLUSION

English is a global language. It is the language of business, diplomacy, finance, science, and technology. In part, its importance can be measured in numbers:

- Over 350 million people speak English as their native language
- An additional 350 million people speak it as their second language
- Half of the world's books are published in English
- 80% of the world's computer text is English

Knowing how to communicate effectively in English will help you succeed both professionally and personally. By learning the building blocks of English and other vocabulary enhancement skills, you can master hundreds of powerful, important words.

You know you have the intelligence, drive, and resilience to succeed. Now, you'll have the fluency with the words you need, too.